T3-AKB-790

Preventive Intervention

in

Social Work

by

Ludwig L. Geismar

Professor of Social Work and Sociology
Rutgers — The State University

The Scarecrow Press, Inc.

Metuchen, N. J.   1969

In Memory of Beverly Ayres

Foreword

What was advocated programmatically a few years ago by a small social work minority is now becoming the dominant reality. Social work sees itself in "normal" institutional, rather than residual, context. It seeks ways to address social institutions as such, while continuing its work with individual, group and community "clients." Developmental provision is acknowledged, in theory at least, as being no less relevant to our function than our remedial and therapeutic measures. In addition to diagnostically-guided case services we advocate universally available "social utilities," accessible at user option or by user status.

This new direction for the profession can be either solidly charted or superficially accommodated. It can swing with the fads of the day or grow out of what we know or can learn. It can be the product only of ideology and politics or can integrate values, social and political goals, knowledge, feasibility and skill. In short, it can strengthen our profession or undercut it.

Ludwig L. Geismar has no question about what the social work tradition requires. Working as he always does modestly and in a circumscribed, significant, area he has given us, in the monograph, an empirical approach to hypothesis development with reference to prevention of family breakdown. One need not endorse all the methodological choices made or conclusions drawn to feel that solid work of this kind, step-by-step fact finding and consideration of possibilities, will pay off for the profession in many ways. On such foundations, much can be built.

Indeed, the completion of the monograph offers occasion to note that the author, alone or on occasion with collaborators, has demonstrated an admirable pattern of basic research and action evaluation over many years. Only an increase in such work by many others will give us the practice theory and knowledge so needed by the social work profession. Whether in Measuring Family Functioning, Understanding the Multi-Problem Family, The Forgotten Neighborhood, several other major monographs and many articles--

or in the present work--we see a careful blending of the
theoretical and the empirical, a willingness to try things
out and to report honestly, as well as a sense of the relevant.   What more can one say than "Godspeed?"

Alfred J. Kahn
Professor of Social Work
Columbia University
School of Social Work

Acknowledgements

The present study was carried out to provide a theoretical and empirical base for the establishment of the Rutgers Family Life Improvement Project, a research-action endeavor on prevention of family disorganization. The project itself, and the writing of this manuscript was made possible by the financial support rendered under HEW 190 by the Social and Rehabilitation Service, formerly known as the Welfare Administration, Department of Health, Education, and Welfare. The collection and analysis of data, carried out by students and teaching assistants of the Rutgers University School of Social Work, was subsidized by National Institute of Mental Health grants 5-Tl-MH7503-02,03.

I owe a debt to the graduate students of my research seminars on Social Functioning and the Family Life Cycle in the academic years 1962/3 and 1963/4 for contributing to the gathering and coding of interviews. The following recipients of NIMH summer research stipends were most helpful in the processing of data: June Garelick, Helen Rudnick, Karen Smith, and Walda Ciafone. I also wish to thank Harriet Fink, Zona Fishkin, Patricia Lagay, and Judy Schwartz for their responsible coding effort, and Mildred Badanes, Anne Cohen, and Barbara Ann Hill for preparing case materials.

Dr. Clarice Stoll and Edward Mednick provided able assistance in the machine analysis of data. I am greatly indebted to June Wells and to Professors Ursula Gerhart and Isabel Wolock for painstaking supervision of the work of several research teams. Mrs. Ann Halkovich, Mrs. Edith D'Amato and Mrs. Gertrude Kleinman were helpful indeed in planning the logistics of sampling in three communities. Thanks are also due to Professor Jane Krisberg for contributing ideas to the writing of Chapter 3.

I am most grateful to Dean Werner W. Boehm for helpful criticism of an earlier draft of the manuscript and to Professors Bruce Lagay and Max Siporin for suggesting modifications of and additions to the present version of the manuscript. They are, however, in no way responsible for any mistakes or shortcomings in the present study.

I wish to extend my appreciation to Mrs. Adele Verzatt for her untiring effort in typing the manuscript. To my wife, Shirley Geismar, goes a special vote of thanks for providing effective editorial assistance. Finally, I should like to acknowledge my debt to the 281 families who participated in this research project. Freely and generously they gave time and information about their lives in the spirit of contributing to the growth of research knowledge.

L. L. G.

Table of Contents

		Page
Foreword by Alfred J. Kahn		v
Acknowledgements		vii
Introduction		11

Chapter

1	The Meaning of Prevention in Social Work	13
2	Family Functioning and Its Correlates	25
3	Research Alternatives for Constructing Models for Preventive Intervention	58
4	Preventive Intervention at Three Levels of Family Functioning - Three Case Studies	83
5	From Remedial to Preventive Intervention	111
Index		127

Introduction

In the field of social work the concept of prevention might be characterized appropriately by Charles Dudley Warner's often quoted witticism: "Everybody talks about the weather, but nobody does anything about it." Prevention is viewed as the most humane and advanced level of service because it is concerned with helping before the occurrence of a problem, an illness, or a pathological condition. The prestigious and non-controversial character of prevention has undoubtedly hindered its development as a serious endeavor in social work more than it has helped. Since all of practice was seen as addressing itself, in one form or another, to the issue of prevention, there seemed to be little reason, conceptually or empirically, for recognizing it as a special type of social work service.

This volume seeks to make preventive social work a part of research and social action, using as its point of departure the premise, accepted by the fields of social work, medicine, public health, and psychiatry, that prevention is desirable and important. This monograph is intended to define the concept of preventive intervention and to apply it to a practice situation in which prevention hypotheses can be tested empirically.

Young families were chosen as the recipients of professional intervention, in the practice situation, for two reasons: first, data already collected in this area lend themselves to the development of a prevention model; and second, preventive intervention with families is given high priority by a profession which finds it increasingly difficult to cope with the consequences of the familial neglect and disorganization which is widespread in our society.

Because of the embryonic nature of conceptualizing and theory building in social work, model building for preventive services is destined to be a slow, drawn-out, process. Existing formulations of preventive intervention have drawn on definitions from the field of public health. They have sought to identify types of services appropriate to conditions and sit-

11

uations assumed to occur prior to the onset of a disease,
of a pathology, or of a social problem. The present study,
in contrast to the existing studies, seeks to relate preventive
planning and knowledge about family development. It attempts
to identify three conditions necessary for defining prevention
operationally and for testing it empirically. These are: (1)
The establishment of a set of rough diagnostic concepts which
describe family functioning on a continuum from a normal to
a problematic or to a pathological situation; (2) The analysis
of evidence, or at least plausible hypotheses, about the relationship between the nature of social functioning and stages of
family development; (3) The description of programs of intervention appropriate to specific levels of social functioning
identified in the process of family development.

The professional social worker is well aware of the
fact that adequate fulfillment of these conditions is a longed-
for goal rather than a present reality. This writer believes
that theory and model building must not limit itself to the
ideal pattern of orderly, step-by-step development but must
proceed in an oscillating manner in which beginning conceptu-
alizations and empirical studies have the opportunity to interact so that they may lead to enrichment of the scientific process.

Chapter 1 discusses the concept of prevention and its
application to the field of social work. Chapter 2, relying
mainly on empirical data, delineates the social functioning of
a representative sample of young families shortly after the
birth of their first child. Chapter 3 examines research alternatives for constructing models of preventive intervention.
Three case studies, illustrating the use of preventive services
at different levels of family functioning, are presented in
Chapter 4. Finally, Chapter 5, after examining some un-
tested assumptions about the merits of preventive intervention, looks at the possible implications of making it a core
service in the social welfare field.

Chapter 1
The Meaning of Prevention
In Social Work

Prevention is generally considered a key concept in medicine and public health. In fact, John D. Porterfield questions whether public health services would have come into existence as a profession if it had not been able to prevent disease. [1] Prevention, according to Alfred J. Kahn, has always been a concern in social work, but he concedes that it is in treatment and control that social workers enjoy the strongest claims as practitioners. [2] During the past few years a number of writings have appeared in the social work literature which reflect current thinking on the subject of prevention. The Social Work Curriculum Study, [3] directed by Werner W. Boehm, included prevention among the functions of social work. The Commission on Social Work Practice of the National Association of Social Workers, in a report entitled Prevention and Treatment, [4] considers ways in which activities directed toward prevention should be organized.

A number of writers in the field of social work have examined the concept of prevention relative to practice[5-14] and have presented diverse points of view regarding the appropriateness of the public health model for social work. Bertram Beck says, cogently, "No matter where the worker is in the spectrum of severity, he is preventing because no matter how trivial or severe the problem is, it can get worse." Beck is saying, in effect, that the concept of intervention as used in the field of social work invariably has a preventive dimension, particularly if we fail to define clearly what is meant by prevention. [15]

Public health has certainly been aware of this issue and has sought to resolve it by differentiating conceptually among primary, secondary, and tertiary prevention. The first is synonymous with intervention before the occurrence of pathology or malfunctioning. The second denotes intervention initiated because of emerging malfunctioning, or treatment dispensed before the disease has run its full course. Tertiary prevention pertains to treatment that is given to

overcome or ameliorate the effects of the disease; this can
be viewed as rehabilitation. There is little question, though,
that reference to prevention in the social work literature pertains mainly to primary prevention or to secondary prevention where malfunctioning is in its beginning stages and can
be dealt with as the result of early detection. This is the
way in which the term prevention will be used in this study.

The argument in the social work literature regarding
the appropriateness of prevention in social work is carried
on at two levels which are not always differentiated. The
first resolves itself into an ideological issue concerning the
desirability of having social work throw its weight behind
what Kahn terms developmental provisions[16] or having it continue instead to emphasize remedial and rehabilitative services. Kahn, in citing Rapoport, notes "that a concern with
prevention is a natural consequence of an institutional view of
social work and social welfare services as normal, basic,
ongoing features of industrial society."[17] To the extent that
American social welfare continues to be characterized by a
"residual"[18] view, prevention plays a minor part in social
work.

At the second level the question of prevention is reduced to a determination of whether the concept is indeed applicable to social work practice. To answer this question it
is necessary to delineate a specific area of practice or of
professional intervention by specifying what it is that needs
preventing, when it needs preventing, how it is to be prevented, and who is to perform the preventive intervention.[19]

This volume seeks to develop a beginning model for
preventive intervention in the single area of social work with
families; i.e., social work aimed at preventing serious family disorganization. The model for preventive intervention
discussed here is currently being tested in the Family Life
Improvement Project, in Newark, N.J. The research design for
testing the feasibility of prevention in social work is discussed elsewhere.[20] This report is devoted largely to designing a model for preventive services, based on an empirical study of family problems and needs. The theoretical and
methodological background of the measurement process used
in the study can be summarized very briefly here as follows:
The key concept used in this discussion is that of family
functioning which has been operationally defined by means of
the St. Paul Scale of Family Functioning.[21] The scale
measures the role performance of family members against

criteria of adequacy in terms of the following four dimensions: a) Whether laws are being violated or observed;
b) Whether behavior contributes to or is harmful to the physical, social, and emotional well-being of family members;
c) Whether behavior is in harmony or conflict with the standards of the family's status group; and d) Whether a family
member's behavior is personally satisfying and commensur-
ate with his potential for social functioning. [22]

The social functioning of a family is in fact measured
in nine areas and twenty-six sub-categories on a continuum
of scores ranging from 7, adequate, to 1, inadequate, social
functioning, with 4, the marginal functioning, in the middle
position.   An acceptable degree of Guttman type scalability
of the St. Paul Scale makes it possible to employ mean
scores for characterizing the nature of a family's social
functioning. [23]   A recent scale validity test, in which the responses from independent interviews with husbands and wives
were compared, yielded very satisfactory results. [24]

The "What" of Prevention

With the social functioning of the family as the chief
dependent variable in family social work, the question of
what needs preventing can now be answered by use of the
concept of serious malfunctioning of the family, or family
disorganization.   If we accept the proposition that adequate
social functioning in the form of social and emotional well-
being, mutuality of role performance, and social acceptance
by others, constitutes a desirable state, we can argue further
that serious family malfunctioning is undesirable and needs
to be prevented.

Various crude indices of family disorganization such
as divorce, desertion, separation, non-support, child neglect,
etc. suggest that the problem is widespread in American society. [25]   Attempts at assessing the prevalence of family malfunctioning by means of a more refined measurement likewise suggest that the social disorganization of the family is
not an isolated phenomenon. [26]   While extreme family disorganization equated with multi-problem behavior might affect
only two to three percent of urban families[27] there is evidence that less severe forms of family disorganization are
more widespread. [28]

Unfortunately, we cannot match our ability to define

family disorganization operationally with precise knowledge
about causation or with interventive skills which, like certain
antibiotics and inoculations, could prevent disease or effect
demonstrable cures. We assume, nonetheless, that our
method of intervention has a measurable effect, and that
early intervention, in particular, will lead to reduced inci-
dence of serious family disorganization and to relatively
more adequate functioning. With the knowledge we have at
this stage, we do not expect prevention in the social work
context to mean the complete elimination of malfunctioning;
rather, we would hope to effect its reduction to a statistically significant degree in the treated as compared with the untreated population.

        Prevention in social work means action or interven-
tion in a population which has not yet manifested signs of
serious malfunctioning but for which it is possible to make
statistical predictions about the occurrence of problem functioning if intervention is not forthcoming. To plan this type
of prevention effectively, some knowledge of the natural
course of family development with regard to social functioning must be gathered, and to this end we shall draw on an
analysis of the social functioning of two suburban family
groups at different stages of the family life cycle. By comparing the differences in social functioning between the two
age cohorts and, in particular, by testing the thesis that
families become more malfunctioning as they grow older, we
may gain the information necessary to chart a possible course
of primary intervention.

        Prevention can also be planned by studying the social
characteristics, the functioning, attitudes and beliefs of a
representative group of young families and thereby gathering
clues from their present behavior about future functioning.
Such an approach is likely to stress secondary rather than
primary prevention, in the sense that interventive planning
would be focussed on areas of emerging malfunctioning. The
empirical data in this study deal initially with the second approach. They analyze a representative sample of urban
families to establish a base line for determining to what extent and in what areas preventive intervention may be appropriate. In a later portion of the study the inter-generational
data, which have a bearing on changes in functioning resulting from family development, will be considered.

The "When" of Prevention

The "When" of prevention involves a set of propositions whose correctness needs ultimate verification by means
of extended research on family functioning. We are stating
these propositions on the basis of preliminary empirical evidence in their favor. The basic proposition set forth here
postulates a direct relationship between social functioning
and the family life cycle. Divorce statistics showing high
rates of family breakup during the first three years of marriage notwithstanding, [29] the fact is that the tentative evidence
from research on lower-class families points to increasing
family disorganization as the family grows older. There are
two reasons why divorce rates per se are not a good index
of family disorganization as herein defined. First, roughly
half of the divorces are granted to childless couples, many
of whom have not been married long, [30] and they do not constitute a family[31] in the sense in which the term is used
here. Second, the high remarriage rate of divorced men and
women[32] reflects discontinuity in family functioning especially
where the succeeding unions are more successful than the
previous ones. A case might even be made for hypothesiz-
ing that early divorce serves to weed out unworkable marriages before they have had a chance to result in serious
family disorganization. [33]

Empirical data supporting a direct relationship between family disorganization and stages of the family life cycle
are still in limited supply at this time. Blood and Wolfe,
using cross-sectional analysis of family groups at different
life cycle stages, found a decline in marital companionship,
love, and general satisfaction in each child-rearing stage until the post parental period. [34] A comparison of two random
samples of families in a New Jersey community revealed
that the older families, with one or more children in junior
high school, were functioning less adequately than the young
families with a first child under one year of age. [35] Other
inferential evidence supporting the contention that malfunctioning becomes more widespread as the family gets older is
the increase in agency registrations for families moving to
the middle stages of the life cycle, indicating a growing and
unmet need for services and resources. [36]

Theoretically speaking, growing family disorganization
may be viewed as an increasing failure on the part of family
members to play their various socially expected roles in a

satisfactory manner. The reasons for this are not altogether clear, but two possible explanations may be advanced at this point: (1) Marriage in Western society in general and the United States in particular is founded on a set of expectations with core values which may be termed romantic love and companionship. Sociologists have long questioned whether the characteristics and expectations that bring people together in marriage are the ones that make for a stable union. While there is unquestionably a gap between the marriage expectations of potential mates and the actual roles played in early married life, it is possible that this gap widens as children are born and the parents are thrust into new roles for which they have had little or no preparation. Growing disorganization would thus represent a progressing discrepancy between the roles the marriage partners are ready to play and are actually filling and the role demands of later family life.

(2) Family disorganization can, furthermore, be viewed, to a large extent, as a function of the fit between family need (defined loosely as a requirement for services and resources) and the availability of these services and resources, as well as a readiness to use them. As the family moves through the early life cycle stages as outlined by Evelyn Duvall, [37] from "beginning families" to "childbearing families" to "families with pre-school children, school children, teenagers, etc.," the need for economic and social resources increases. Consequently the family's economic, social, and emotional resources are put under a heavier strain and where these resources are limited, family disorganization is likely to result.

If family disorganization does indeed grow more severe as the family advances in age, that suggests that early professional intervention at a stage of lesser disorganization might be more effective than later intervention. This thought is presented as a common sense notion without any empirical support from social work research. We are merely applying here a widely accepted medical principle which holds that a mild disease is generally more amenable to treatment than one that is more severe. Carrying this analogy to family life, it might be argued that deficiencies in social functioning which have not yet led to a breakdown in communication or to sharply deviant behavior can be treated more easily and probably with more success than deficiencies which have set into motion whole patterns of problematic behavior.

It is, nonetheless, important to point out that while prevention in public health means action to keep a disease or state of pathology from occurring, social malfunctioning is unlike most preventable diseases, for it is not readily subject to total prevention. It is probably present, to a mild degree at least, in most family situations and, unfortunately, the most highly skilled intervention does not have the potency of vaccines or quarantine. Early intervention in family functioning, then, means the rendering of appropriate service either to prevent malfunctioning if none has indeed occurred, or to eliminate, ameliorate or control limited malfunctioning. All four measures are designed to prevent social malfunctioning from reaching, through cumulative growth, the proportions of family disorganization. In the instances where this has already occurred, intervention early in the life cycle of the malfunction is designed to effect a reduction in malfunctioning.

The "How" of Prevention

The "How" of prevention is our main subject. Intervention for enhancing social functioning, whether remedial or preventive, is, of course, the stock-in-trade of the social work profession. A skilled social worker is not likely to be at a loss when asked to develop a treatment plan based upon a diagnostic evaluation of a family. The approach proposed here differs in one important aspect from the more routine procedure of case diagnosis and treatment planning. We are trying to put forth a plan of treatment that is not designed for a particular case but for a large group of cases. Instead of designing a treatment plan based upon the social diagnosis of a specific family, we seek to develop a plan geared to the needs of an entire group of families for whom the treatment is intended.

There is, of course, not any one treatment plan that fits a great number of families--a point which rests upon the implicit assumption that an effective plan needs to be fitted closely to the diagnosis of each case. Yet we make the further assumption that, in spite of an infinite variation among a large number of families, all of them share some common characteristics and that these characteristics can be used to establish a collective treatment plan, which we shall call a model. The first step for the researcher is to enumerate these shared characteristics; in keeping with accepted research procedures their number can be maximized by proper grouping and categorizing. The result will be a grouping along specified shared dimensions as the latter might be relevant to a given treatment plan. Having once established groups of families which differ from each other on certain relevant and, hopefully, related characteristics, it is possible to view the groupings as empirical types--that is, types derived from the distribution of characteristics in an actual sample of cases. These types need not be completely uniform. They should show certain modal patterns of behavior along a specified dimension (which is family functioning, in our case). Moreover, we should find a number of other psycho-social characteristics associated with the major property which characterizes each type. Hence, each empirical type will represent a cluster of correlated characteristics which have relevance for treatment planning. The treatment plan in itself may then constitute a projected course of intervention which has a high probability of appropriateness in a maximum number of situations.

This treatment plan, which we have termed a model, should be applicable to clusters of family characteristics, but it does not yield an exact blueprint for intervention in every case. It is, rather, a statement of the major treatment approach seen as most appropriate to the combination of modal characteristics found in each family type. Because the model does not envisage an individual fitting of case and intervention method but pertains rather to a collection of both, it is necessarily general (i. e. nonspecific) in character and projects strategy of intervention rather than tactics.

No treatment techniques are provided in the last chapter of this book, which outlines the strategy of intervention. Hopefully, these techniques can be specified in the process of carrying out an actual program of preventive services, using the broad strategy of intervention as its framework. [38]

Notes

1.   John D. Porterfield, M. D. "Public Health Goals," Public Health Concepts in Social Work Education. New York, Council on Social Work Education, 1962. pp. 18-26; p. 22.

2.   Alfred J. Kahn, "Therapy Prevention and Developmental Provisions, A Social Work Strategy," Public

Health Concepts in Social Work Education. New York,
Council on Social Work Education, 1962. pp. 132-148.

3. Werner W. Boehm, Objectives of the Social Work
    Curriculum Study. New York, Council on Social
    Work Education, 1959. p. 51.

4. National Association of Social Workers, Commission
    on Social Work Practice, "Prevention and Treatment."
    New York, 1959. (Mimeographed working draft.)

5. Florence E. Cyr and Shirley H. Wattenberg, "Social
    Work in a Preventive Program of Maternal and Child
    Health." Social Work, Vol. II, No. 3, July 1957,
    pp. 32-38.

6. Bradley Buell, "Is Prevention Possible?" Community
    Organization 1959. New York, Columbia University
    Press, 1959. pp. 3-18.

7. Bertram Beck, "Can Social Work Prevent Social
    Problems." Social Welfare Forum 1960. New York,
    Columbia University Press 1960. pp. 180-193.

8. Council on Social Work Education, Concepts of Pre-
    vention and Control: Their Use in the Social Work
    Curriculum. New York, Council on Social Work Edu-
    cation 1961.

9. Lydia Rapoport, "Concept of Prevention in Social
    Work." Social Work, Vol. VI, No. 1, January 1961,
    pp. 3-12.

10. Milton Wittman, "Preventive Social Work: A Goal for
    Practice and Education." Social Work, Vol. VI, No.
    1, January, 1961, pp. 19-28.

11. Berta Fantl, "Preventive Intervention." Social Work,
    Vol. VII, No. 3, July, 1962, pp. 41-47.

12. Lydia Rapoport, "Working with Families in Crisis,
    An Exploration in Preventive Intervention." Social
    Work, Vol. VII, No. 3, July, 1962, pp. 4-47.

13. Howard J. Parad, "Preventive Casework: Problems
    and Implications." Crisis Intervention: Selected
    Readings, ed. Howard J. Parad. New York Family

Service Association of America 1965. pp. 284-298.

14.   Florence Haselkorn, "An Ounce of Prevention."
Journal of Education for Social Work, Vol. III, No.
2 Fall, 1967, pp. 61-70.

15.   Beck, op. cit. p. 181.

16.   Kahn, op. cit. pp. 145-147.

17.   Ibid., p. 137.

18.   Stated briefly the residual view sees welfare come
into play mainly when the basic institutions of society
such as the family and economy fail to meet human
need. The institutional conception assigns a role to
social welfare, "a proper, legitimate function of mod-
ern industrial society in helping individual achieve
self fulfillment."
Harold A. Wilensky and Charles N. Lebeaux, Industrial Society and Social Welfare. New York, Russell
Sage Foundation, 1958. pp. 138-140.

19.   The "what," "when," and "how" is discussed in this
chapter, while the "who" is dealt with in Chapter 2.

20.   "Family Life Improvement Project--Research Action
on Prevention of Family Disorganization" (Graduate
School of Social Work, Rutgers-The State University,
New Brunswick, N.J.). (Mimeographed) Copies are
available upon request. The project is sponsored by
the Welfare Administration as Grant HEW 190.

21.   L. L. Geismar and Beverly Ayres, Measuring Family
Functioning, A Manual on a Method for Evaluating
the Social Functioning of Disorganized Families.
St. Paul, Minn., Family Centered Project 1960.
L. L. Geismar and Michael LaSorte, Understanding
the Multi-Problem Family, A Conceptual Analysis
and Exploration in Early Identification. New York,
Association Press, 1964.
L. L. Geismar, Michael LaSorte and Beverly Ayres,
"Measuring Family Disorganization." Marriage and
Family Living, Vol. XXIV, No. 1, Feb., 1962,
pp. 51-56.
L. L. Geismar, "Family Functioning as an Index of
Need for Welfare Services." Family Process, Vol.

III, No. 1 (March, 1964), pp. 99-113.
David Wallace, "The Chemung County Evaluation of
Casework Services to Dependent Multi-Problem Fami-
lies." The Social Service Review, Vol. 41, No. 4
Dec., 1967, pp. 379-389.

22.   Geismar, op. cit., p. 101.

23.   Geismar, LaSorte and Ayres, op. cit.

24.   Family Life Improvement Project--Progress Report
       1968. Graduate School of Social Work, Rutgers-The
       State University, New Brunswick, N. J. (Mimeo-
       graphed.)

25.   William J. Goode, The Family. Englewood Cliffs,
       N. J., Prentice-Hall, Inc., p. 91-102.   William F.
       Kenkel, The Family in Perspective.   New York,
       Appleton-Century-Crofts, 1960, pp. 287-318.   Eliza-
       beth Meier, "Child Neglect." Social Work and Social
       Problems, ed. Nathan E. Cohen.   New York, Na-
       tional Association of Social Workers, 1964, pp. 153-
       200.   Helen R. Jeter, Children, Problems, and Serv-
       ices in Child Welfare Programs.   Department of
       Health, Education and Welfare, 1963.

26.   Beverly Ayres and Joseph C. Lagey, Checklist Sur-
       vey of Multi-Problem Families in Vancouver City.
       Vancouver, Community Chest and Councils of
       Greater Vancouver Area, March, 1961. (Mimeo-
       graphed.)
       L. L. Geismar, Report on a Checklist Survey.   St.
       Paul, Minn., Family Centered Project, 1957. (Mim-
       eographed.)

27.   Geismar and LaSorte, op. cit., pp. 52-93.

28.   Ibid., p. 57.

29.   After the first few months of marriage the risk of
       divorce quickly rises to reach a maximum during the
       third year.   Thereafter, the divorce rate begins to
       drop.   William J. Goode, "Family Disorganization,"
       Contemporary Social Problems, ed. Robert K. Mer-
       ton and Robert Nesbit.   New York, Harcourt, Brace
       and World, 1961, pp. 411-12.

30.   William F. Kenkel, The Family in Perspective.
       New York, Appleton-Century-Crofts, Inc., 1960,
       p. 335.

31.   We are using the term family to mean one or two
       parents or parent substitutes who have assumed re-
       sponsibility for one or more dependent children.

32.   Thomas P. Monahan, citing several sources, esti-
       mates that perhaps as many as three-fourths of all
       divorcees remarry.   Thomas P. Monahan, "The
       Changing Nature and Instability of Remarriages."
       Selected Studies in Marriage and the Family, Robert
       F. Winch et al. (Revised edition.) New York, Holt
       Rinehart and Winston, 1962, pp. 627-635.

33.   This is admittedly a controversial point and evidence
       to support the above thesis is lacking.   Thomas P.
       Monahan cites two contradictory prevailing points of
       view on the stability of remarriage following divorce.
       His own research in Iowa indicates a higher divorce
       rate among remarrying divorcees than among those
       married for the first time.   Other researchers, us-
       ing happiness and adjustment as a criterion of suc-
       cess, found divorcees doing better in their second
       marriage than in the first.   Ibid.

34.   Robert O. Blood and Donald M. Wolfe, Husbands
       and Wives. New York, The Free Press, 1960.

35.   This study is reported below.   Parallel evidence is
       contained in a comparison of middle-aged and young
       families, with the latter showing more adequate func-
       tioning in intra-familial areas than the former.
       Walda Ciafone et al, "Relationship of Family Func-
       tioning to Anomie, Social Class and Other Related
       Factors." (Unpublished MSW thesis, Graduate School
       of Social Work, Rutgers-The State University, June,
       1963.)

36.   Geismar and LaSorte, op. cit., pp. 60-64.

37.   Evelyn M. Duvall, Family Development.   Chicago,
       J. B. Lippincott Co., 1957, chapters 6-14.

38.   Family Life Improvement Project, op. cit.

Chapter 2
Family Functioning and Its Correlates

Nature of the Study Population

Since we are developing a model for intervention aimed at preventing family disorganization, it is axiomatic that the study population be made up of families functioning satisfactorily. This requirement makes the clientele of social agencies unsuitable as subjects since they already exhibit evidences of malfunctioning. The logical study sample was a target group composed of young families showing patterns of social functioning within the normal range found in the average community. The study itself would reveal the precise pattern of "normalcy." However, general knowledge about family behavior suggested that a randomly selected group of urban families would include a small proportion of cases characterized by severe social disorganization.

The population selected for the study was a group of families similar to that included in the treatment program of the Rutgers Family Life Improvement Project. The Project sample was not included in the present research since the latter effort, devoted to developing a treatment model, necessarily preceded the preventive intervention study. The research sample, similar in character to the project sample, was composed of young two- or single-parent families with a first dependent child born within a year of the interview, to a mother under thirty years of age. The families represented a probability sample selected from the vital statistics register of three New Jersey communities: Newark, Plainfield, and New Brunswick. The latter two were selected to study the possible effects upon family functioning of small city and quasi-suburban living (both communities have populations of approximately 40,000 and are located on the fringes of the New York-Newark metropolitan area) as against metropolitan living (Newark's population is about 400,000). Newark cases comprised a 10% random sample of first births in the first eight months of 1962. New Brunswick and Plainfield cases, by contrast, covered all the first births during the first eight months of 1963. The combined

sample of 216 respondents is made up of 78 Newark families, 61 New Brunswick families, and 77 Plainfield families.
These respective N's are only about 50% of the names drawn
in the sample.   Allowing for some variations among the
communities, the heavy attrition rate can be accounted for
largely as follows: family moved out of the area, 20-30%;
family could not be found at home, [1] 5-15%; family refused
to be interviewed, 2-12%; and address listed was unknown
or family was not known to have lived at the address listed,
3-10%.

    We had no reliable way of testing the nature of the
differences between cases which were interviewed and those
which were missed.   In the Newark sample we found a
similar proportion of Negroes among the families interviewed (46%) as in the total universe of first births to
mothers under thirty years of age (48%). [2] In a subsequent
sample of 600 young Newark families selected in the same
manner as the present sample, a comparison was made between cases interviewed and cases missed (again roughly
fifty percent of the original sample drawn) on such demo-
graphic properties as race, legitimacy of birth, occupation-
al status of the husband, assorted characteristics of the
neighborhood, and median dollar gross rental of the census
tract. [3]   No striking differences were found between the two
groups on these variables.   In short, our natural concern
over the high sample attrition was somewhat ameliorated by
evidence that the families on whom we collected data were
not radically different on two significant variables from the
larger population from which the sample was drawn. [4]

    The aforementioned sample of young families, which
we hope are representative of urban and suburban families
at the beginning of the family life cycle, served then as the
source of research data for our effort to sketch a tentative
preventive intervention model.

Types of Research Data Collected

    Even a generalized model for a strategy of interven-
tion must fully take into account those aspects of behavior,
attitudes, values, and environment which are the basis for
judging a family as adequate and well able to manage their
lives, or problematic and in need of professional help. Toward this end three kinds of data were collected on the
families interviewed:

(1) Past and present family functioning, using an expanded version of the St. Paul Scale of Family Functioning. The sample comprises 216 young and 65 older families. (2) Family values and goals of the mother, with special reference to the child rearing, marital and parental roles, by means of ten PARI scales.[5] (3) The mother's feeling of social integration vs. alienation, by means of the Srole Anomie Scale.[6] The data on family functioning were procured with the aid of two-hour to three-hour open ended interviews conducted with the mother in her home. The PARI and Anomie scales, structured, self-administered questionnaires, were completed by the mothers themselves except in cases where reading problems made it necessary for the interviewer to read the questions and check the answers given by the respondent.

Basic Social Characteristics
of the Study Population

Demographically 65. 7% of the 216 young families are white,[7] 32. 4% Negro, and 1. 9% (four families) are racially mixed. The religious distribution is as follows: 44. 4% Protestant, 31. 0% Catholic, 10. 2% Jewish. Other religions and religiously mixed marriages make up 14. 4% of the sample. Eighty-one percent of the families were, at the time of the interview, headed by married couples, 18. 1% by unwed mothers and in . 9% (two cases) the marital status of the family was unclear.

The very nature of the sample set the age of mothers under or barely above thirty at the time of the interview. Her median age was twenty whereas that of the father was twenty-two at the time of marriage. Seventy percent of the women and 69% of the men either finished high school or continued their education beyond it, but only 3. 7% of the women as against 7. 9% of the men had never attended high school. Occupationally, the sample families were spread over all the major census categories with the highest concentration in the following groupings: unskilled laborer, 30%; skilled laborer, 16%; clerical and sales, 13. 0%; professional, 12. 0%. Of the remaining 29%: there was no information on 12%; 5% worked as foremen; 4% were unemployed; and the other 8% were divided among low level managerial, semi-professional, and college student. Nearly eighty percent of the women stayed home with their children; the remainder worked, for the most part in unskilled occupations.

Slightly over half the men and a little under half the women were born in the sample cities or in the State of New Jersey. Of the remainder, roughly equal proportions of men and women listed their birthplaces as Northern and Eastern U.S.A. other than New Jersey (18%) and Southern United States (19%). Others were born in the American Midwest or Far West, Puerto Rico, Canada, Latin America, Europe, and miscellaneous countries of the other continents.

The modal living arrangement for the families was a private apartment (73.6%). Other forms of housing were house ownership (10.6%), housekeeping room (7.9%), house rental (3.7%), and public housing project (2.3%). No information was available on four cases (1.9%).

In 67.1% of the cases studied the young family of procreation lived alone. A variety of other living arrangements, with parents and relatives, was found. The most common of these alternate housing arrangements had the young family living with the man's or the woman's (split about evenly) family of orientation (11.6%), and the mother and child (usually out-of-wedlock) living with her parents (10.6%). The remaining 10.7% represented a variety of miscellaneous living arrangements.

In only two of the families (0.9%) the man and in five families (2.3%) the woman had had a prior marriage, while the vast bulk--two hundred cases (92.6%)--represented either first marriages or out-of-wedlock situations. In nine situations (4.2%) information on prior marital status was missing.

In nearly half of these young families, or 46.3%, their first child was born between nine and twenty-four months after marriage. But in 16.2% of the cases (excluding out-of-wedlock situations) the first born arrived less than nine months after the wedding date. Three children were born before the wedding. The rest of the families showed the following timing of births relative to the date of the marriage: In 5.1% of study families, the first child was born between 25-30 months after the wedding; in 6% it was born between 31-36 months following that event; and in 6.4% that baby arrived more than three years after marriage. Out-of-wedlock births amounted to 18.1% of families studied, and precise information was missing on 1.9% of the cases.

The Social Functioning of Young Families

When discussing the social functioning of young families, it is well to recall that we are discussing the manner in which a mother-father-baby triad or a mother (or mother surrogate)-baby dyad carries out a variety of socially expected tasks. These have as their objectives providing family members with physical, social, and emotional satisfaction; with shelter and security; imparting a sense of identity and belongingness; and socializing children. Interviews with 216 families who are reasonably representative of the young, urban, married population yielded narrative data which permitted a rating on adequacy of functioning by the criteria of the St. Paul Scale of Family Functioning.

The data obtained are the product of single interviews. Although the interviews were done, for the most part, by social work students with some interviewing experience and skill, they were not based upon a therapeutic or close social relationship. Therefore, we feel justified in assuming that a certain amount of deviant or stigmatized behavior went unreported. On the other hand, the home visits made by the interviewer, the discussion and questionnaire data procured by them, and the observations made during the two-hour to three-hour interview yielded a wealth of information which permitted a reasonably objective characterization of families in terms of social status, economic situation, nature of housekeeping, health of family members, social participation, use of community resources, values, goals, etc. Even allowing for some underreporting and distortion in the area of inter- and intrapsychic functioning, we are led to believe that people with problems were generally eager to share them with, rather than keep them from, the interviewer. [8]

Evidence on the reliability of the St. Paul Scale is given in publications listed in footnote 21 of Chapter 1. The most comprehensive data on reliability and validity of this form of measurement were produced in the Chemung County Research Demonstration With Dependent Multi-Problem Families, which investigated the degree to which separate teams of coders were consistent in rating the same set of family functioning data, and correlated results with those obtained by use of the Hunt-Kogan Movement Scale. [9]

Other evidence on the validity of data was obtained by separate interviewing of ten wives and their husbands in this

research sample and then comparing the interview results
with their social functioning ratings on the seven point continuum of the St. Paul Scale.   The results, showing a high
measure of agreement between husband and wife on the nature of their family's functioning, are given in Table I.

Table 1

Husband and Wife Agreement
on Level of Family Functioning

	No. of responses	Percent
Complete agreement	47	58. 8
Conditional agreement Ratings 1 Scale Point Apart	27	33. 7
Disagreement Ratings 2 or more Scale Points Apart	6	7. 5
Total	80	100. 0

In measuring a cross section of young, urban families,
the St. Paul Scale of Family Functioning, which was set up
to measure serious family disorganization, discriminates
more sharply at the lower (or malfunctioning) end of the continuum.   When we designate a family's functioning as Adequate (the upper portion of the scale) we do not mean a situation free of problems.   Rather, the designation Adequate
covers a continuum of conditions ranging from one which may
indeed be problem free to one in which a number of problems are encountered and handled realistically. [10]   Thus Adequate functioning pertains to the external social situation and
the family's ability to cope with daily problems.   Slightly
more than half the young families, 111 or 51. 4% in our
sample of 216, were found to fall in the Adequate group.
This means all areas of family functioning[11] were rated as
Adequate (or assigned a value of seven on the St. Paul
Scale).

Table 2

The Social Function of Sample Families in 8 Areas
of Family Functioning by Problem Groups

Area of Family Functioning	Overall Social Functioning Problematic N=16 Level of Functioning -%			Overall Social Functioning Near Problematic N=29 Level of Functioning -%			Overall Social Functioning Near Adequate N=59 Level of Functioning -%		
	Prob.*	Near Adequate* Adequate*	Adequate*	Prob.	Near Adequate Adequate	Adequate	Prob.	Near Adequate Adequate	Adequate
Family Relationship & Unity	87	6	7	55	31	14	8	38	54
Individual Behavior & Adjustment	56	38	6	24	45	31	0	31	69
Care & Training of Children	29	35	36	7	21	72	0	7	93
Social Activities	25	44	31	11	32	57	0	27	73
Economic Practices	31	38	31	20	16	64	0	25	75
Household Practices	50	12	38	11	20	69	0	19	81
Health Practices	6	6	88	0	11	89	0	7	93
Use of Community Resources	0	33	67	7	4	89	0	14	86

* By the dimensions of the St. Paul Scale of Family Functioning Problematic denotes scores of 5 or less (1-5), Near Adequate indicates a rating of 6, and Adequate a rating of 7.

The designation Near Adequate is used here to denote functioning which is somewhat problematic (assigned a value of six in one to three areas) or considerably problematic (assigned a value of five or less) in one area. The Near Adequately functioning families have encountered problems which have put some strain on the family system but have not posed any threat or disorganization. Fifty-nine or 27. 3% of our families were rated in the Near Adequate group. Family Relationships and Unity emerges as a problematic area in 8% of these families, but social functioning is somewhat less than Adequate in between one third and one fourth of the cases in the areas of Individual Behavior and Adjustment, Social Activities, and Economic Practices. [12]

The next lower group in the social functioning continuum is the Near Problematic. These families show functioning which is somewhat problematic in four to eight areas or quite problematic in two or three areas. Near Problematic families are still several steps removed from a state of disorganization, although in contrast to the Near Adequate group they either face more difficult environmental circumstances or have less ability to cope with problems. Twenty-nine families or 13. 4% of the sample were in the Near Problematic category. Fifty-five percent of these cases have problems in Family Relationships and Unity and 24% show some difficulty in Individual Behavior and Adjustment, for either one or more family members. In Economic Practices twenty percent of the families are encountering problems of various kinds, while 11% or fewer of the families are seen as problematic in other areas of family functioning.

The bottom group of families in the sample is designated as Problematic. These families function at a level below the Near Problematic Group and reveal considerable malfunctioning in four or more areas. This category actually covers a wide spectrum of situations ranging from the truly multi-problem family to cases in which most areas are characterized by malfunctioning slightly above the level of marginal performance (i. e. behavior potentially threatening to the welfare of family members and/or society). [13] Sixteen families or 7. 4% of the sample were classified as Problematic. One case or . 5% of the sample could not be rated or categorized in one of the four problem groups because of insufficient information. Family Relationships and Unity gives difficulty in 87% of the Problematic group of cases, and Individual Behavior and Adjustment was rated as problematic in 56% of them. Household Practices is a mat-

ter of concern in half the group mainly because of poor housing conditions.   Economic Practices are unsatisfactory in
about one-third of these families, again largely as a result
of economic deprivation.   Care and Training of Children and
Social Activities were noted as being problematic in 29% and
25% of the cases respectively, but only 6% of the Problematic groups were affected by problems in the health area--a
fact which reflects the youth of family members.   Use of
Community Resources, while less than satisfactory for a
third of the families, was problematic for none.

This four-fold classification, based upon a score
grouping of measures obtained with the aid of the St. Paul
Scale of Family Functioning, reflects quantitative differences
in the nature of a continuum.   The St. Paul Scale is stan-
dardized for problem families with a mid-point placed at the
marginal value (4 on a 7 point continuum).   Since the group
measured here is a randomly selected population of young
families, among whom a large portion function normally, the
graphic percentage distribution is skewed as shown in Figure
I.

Figure I

Nature of Social Functioning of 216 Young Families

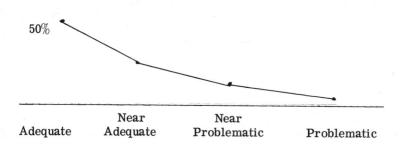

A few generalizations emerge from this distribution.
These young families, in contrast to older families which
have been previously studied with the aid of the St. Paul
Scale, appear to be a relatively well functioning group. [14]
Only four families or less than two percent[15] revealed pat-

terns of functioning close to the marginal level which could
be viewed as potentially multi-problem. In these particular
families problematic functioning was very pronounced in the
areas of Family Relationships, Individual Behavior and Adjustment, Economic Practices, and Home and Household
Practices. But all the sixteen families classified here as
Problematic show evidence of malfunctioning in inter-person-
al behavior and in one or the other of the instrumental
areas, especially in the maintenance of their home and in
making a living. Near Problematic families face problems
largely in family relationships and individual behavior and
to a much lesser extent in economic functioning. The chief
problem area for Near Adequate families is that of family
relationships.

By and large, the young families in the study have
no health problems. They make very restricted use of community resources but this is not an area of concern at this
stage of the family life cycle. At the same time, the mothers are unacquainted with health or welfare agencies which
they might use if the need arises in the future, a significant circumstance which will be discussed later under the
subject of intervention.

The current relationship to parents and in-laws was
described as amicable with frequent meetings for 38% of
the men's families and 60% of the women's families, minor
conflict with frequent meetings for six percent of the men's
families and five percent of the women's families. Infre-
quent but amicable contacts or minor conflicts were noted
for 31% of the men's and 27% of the women's families. The
mothers who were interviewed reported major conflicts or
broken contacts with nine percent of the men's and four percent of the women's parents. Four percent of the relationships with the families of the mothers could not be coded.
Sixteen percent of the relationships with the man's family of
orientation fall under the heading "no contact" because the
child was out-of-wedlock or the data did not permit coding.

It is of some interest to note that only 31. 5% of
these first births in our sample families were said to be
actually planned, while the mothers reported that 63% of all
first births and about 55% of births in-wedlock were unplanned. Five and one-half percent lacked information on
that aspect of the family history. It is not surprising,
therefore, to find that of the 126 mothers who reported on
the use of birth control 73 or 57. 9% said that it had not

been used. In spite of the absence of family planning only
about twenty percent of the married couples evinced a negative attitude toward pregnancy, while the children, once
born, were almost without exception positively accepted by
their mothers.

Data on family goals gathered from all but 12 mothers
in the study sample lent itself to coding.   The 204 mothers
who responded gave 369 responses, or a total of 1. 81 per
interview.   Most mothers (65. 7%) expressed a wish for improved housing.   In fact, the typical goal for the majority
of these families is a house of their own in the suburbs.
The next frequent goal expressed (27. 5% of the women) is a
good education for their children.   Nearly a quarter
(22. 5%)[16] of the mothers stressed financial security as an
important goal, while a fifth of the group expressed a desire for more children.   Other goals listed by ten percent
or fewer of the respondents included a happy home life[17]
and an education for the husband or wife.

The sample is almost evenly divided between regular
churchgoers and couples who never attend church   (about
32% of the cases in each group).   In the rest of the families the couple occasionally attends (12%) or one of the partners, or the single mother, attends services alone (25%).

The preceding account of the families' social characteristics and their present social functioning supports the
contention that as a group young families with a first child
are not a problem-ridden population.   This is not to say
that they are free of problems, for evidence of difficulties
emerged throughout this report in such indices as poor family relationships, marginal economic functioning, inadequate
housing, out-of-wedlock status, conflict with parents and in-
laws, etc.   The distribution of family functioning scores
suggests that a portion of the families are characterized by
malfunctioning in several areas, and although few of these
particular families are truly disorganized or multi-problem,
their group pattern of behavior contrasts clearly with the
adequately functioning families constituting the bulk--about
one-half--of the research sample.

The existence of a range of functioning patterns, from
Adequate to Problematic, together with some situational and
attitudinal correlates enables us to view family functioning
in its broader psycho-social context.   This we shall do in
the succeeding sections of this volume, emphasizing those

factors which may be helpful in suggesting appropriate
strategies of intervention.

Family Functioning and Social Class

The almost consistently negative correlation of many
kinds of physical and mental illness, deviant behavior or social deprivation with social status makes it consistent and
certainly not far-fetched for the researcher to look for a
nexus, more specifically a positive relationship, between social class and family functioning. [18] Here we are inclined to
hypothesize that lower-class existence limits the economic
and educational means required for playing socially expected
roles.   This would apply especially to the roles of income
provider and homemaker, but limitations in these areas are
likely to have an effect on family interactions and relationships to the community as well.

We used a modification of the Hollingshead Index of
Social Position[19] to determine the social class[20] of sample
families.   The modification converts the three-factor scale
into one composed of two factors[21] (based on education and
occupation of family head) and divides a population into six
status categories.   In the present study we employed a
three-fold status grouping (combining Classes I and II, III
and IV, V and VI) in analyzing our sample, referring to them
as High, Medium and Low.   For statistical convenience and
because of the relatively small number of Near Problematic
and Problematic cases, the variable family functioning is divided in most tables into two categories: Adequate and
Less than Adequate.   In some tables, where appropriate, the
categories Adequate, Near Adequate, and Problem Disposed
(a combination of Near Problematic and Problematic) are
used.   The cross-tabulation of social class and family functioning is shown in Table 3.

There is every indication that family functioning is
correlated with social status.   A chi square of 14.91 (2 d.f.,
$p < .01$) reveals that the relationship is statistically significant at the 1% level, or that in one hundred successive random samples fewer than one would yield a different association between the two variables. [22] The contingency coefficient
(a measure of association derived from chi square and de-
noted by C) of .26 shows, nonetheless, that the association
between class and social functioning is of a low magnitude.
Inspection of Table 3 reveals indeed that differences in fam-

Table 3

Relationship Between Social Class and Family Functioning

Percent of Families in Each Social Class

Family Functioning	High	Medium	Low
Adequate	68. 0	67. 2	40. 9
Less than Adequate	32. 0	32. 8	59. 1
Total Percent	100. 0	100. 0	100. 0
N's*	25	70	110

*Where the total N is less than 216 information on one or more of the variables had been found missing.

ily functioning are much more pronounced between the Medium and Low than between the High and Medium status groups. About two-thirds of the High and Medium status groups showed adequate family functioning, but only 40. 9% of the Low group were in the Adequate category. By contrast, less than a third of the upper status families as against 59% of the lower status families were functioning below the adequate level. In other words the chances are about 60 out of 100 that the Low status family is functioning below the adequate level; for High and Medium status families the chances are 33 out of 100.

As stated earlier, respondents in the sample were chosen from one large (Newark) and two small (New Brunswick and Plainfield) urban communities. In a culture which has come to idealize suburban and small town living, much has been said and written about the supposedly wholesome effect of such living upon the health and happiness of residents, in contrast to life in the large city. Extensive research would be required to determine exactly what different people mean when they refer to the positive effects resulting from small town living. In the absence of good theory, we are seeking evidence here in support of this myth, inquiring more specifically whether the large city with widespread slums and high rate of unemployment has a negative effect upon family functioning. When posed in this form the question receives an answer in Table 4.

Table 4

Relationship Between Residence and Family Functioning

Percent of Families in Each Community

Family Functioning	Newark	New Brunswick	Plainfield
Adequate	39. 0	60. 7	56. 6
Less than Adequate	61. 0	39. 3	43. 4
Total Percent	100. 0	100. 0	100. 0
N's in each community	(77)	(61)	(76)

The percentage distribution shows some differences in family functioning between Newark and suburban or small-town residents, indicating more problematic functioning on the part of the Newark residents. The greater similarity between families in the two small cities as compared with Newark families is obvious, and the differences in family functioning among residents of the three communities are statistically significant (X^2 = 7. 72 2 d. f. , p < . 05). However, the question arises whether differences between metropolitan area and small city residents are due to differences in social class.

Table 5 below shows that Newark, compared with New Brunswick and Plainfield, had fewer High and more Low status families. The differences are statistically significant (X^2 = 11. 26, 4 d. f. , p < . 05) at the five percent level, and they appear to reflect the class differences in the population of young families with a first child in the three communities.

Do differences in class distribution among the three communities serve to explain the differences in family functioning? This question can be answered by correlating community and family functioning while holding class constant. The results are shown in Table 6.

Table 6 shows that by controlling for class we do not entirely eliminate differences in social functioning between metropolitan and suburban families. In the High-Medium as

Table 5

Social Class of Families in Three Communities

Social Class	Percent of Families in Each Community		
	Newark	New Brunswick	Plainfield
High	6. 5	15. 3	13. 9
Medium	24. 7	33. 9	43. 05
Low	68. 8	50. 8	43. 05
Total Percent	100. 0	100. 0	100. 0
N in each community*	(77)	(59)	(72)

* Reduction in N's is due to the absence of class data for some families.

Table 6

Relationship Between Residence and Family Functioning with Class Held Constant

SOCIAL CLASS

Family Functioning	High and Medium Percent of Families in Each Community			Low Percent of Families in Each Community		
	Newark	New Brunswick	Plain-field	Newark	New Brunswick	Plain-field
Adequate	54. 2	75. 9	70. 7	34. 0	50. 0	45. 2
Less than Adequate	45. 8	24. 1	29. 3	66. 0	50. 0	54. 8
Total Percent	100. 0	100. 0	100. 0	100. 0	100. 0	100. 0
N's in each community	24	29	41	53	30	31

well as the Low status categories small city families show
more adequate functioning.   However, chi squares comparing metropolitan with New Brunswick and Plainfield families
in upper and lower status groups are below statistical significance (X^2 = 2.98 and 2.24, 2 d.f.; p's fall short of 5%
level of significance).   A comparison of Newark families
with the combined suburban groups likewise does not yield
statistically significant differences in family functioning in
either class.   It may thus be concluded that differences in
family functioning between families living in Newark and
those residing in smaller cities are to a large extent a function of the class differences of the two populations studied.

Examining the interrelationship of class, residence,
and family functioning from the other direction, we find
that class remains a crucial variable in family functioning
even when place of residence is controlled.   When correlating social status of the families with their level of functioning for each one of the communities separately, we obtain
a positive relationship which is statistically significant for
New Brunswick and Plainfield (X^2 4.19 and 4.65, 1 d.f., p =
< .05) but slightly below the 95% confidence level in the
case of Newark (X^2 2.73, 1 d.f., p < .10).   The underrepre-
sentation of High status families in Newark appears to be
largely responsible for the lower statistical significance of
the Newark data.

By way of summary we observe that social class is
indeed positively associated with the level of social functioning of young urban families.   Place of residence, although correlated with this variable as well, ceases to be a
major factor in family functioning once the class factor is
held constant.   Hence the differences between metropolitan
and suburban communities can be explained largely as a result of differences in social stratification.

Family Functioning and Marital Status

It will surprise no one to see marital status significantly correlated with family functioning.   The unmarried
mothers, representing 18% of our sample, came mostly
from deprived homes and lived under economically restric-
tive circumstances.   Twenty-eight of the 34 mothers for
whom we had social status data[23] were classified as belonging to the Low status group.   An approximation of the overall association between marriage and family functioning is

indicated by a coefficient of contingency of .41 and a chi square of 43.44, 2 d.f., p <.001).

Since class is a key factor underlying marital status and is also, as we learned earlier, related to family functioning, it is natural to question whether marital status is related to functioning when class is held constant. Because of the negligible number of cases in the Medium (4) and High (2) categories, we confine our analysis to the Low group, obtaining the relationship shown in Table 7.

Table 7

Relationship Between Family Functioning and
Marital Status in Class V and VI (Low)

| Family Functioning | Percent by Marital Status | |
	Married	Unmarried
Adequate	53.5	3.6
Near Adequate	26.7	46.4
Problem Disposed*	19.8	50.0
Total Percent	100.0	100.0
N's	86	28

* Combines the categories Near Problematic and
Problematic

It is clear from the above table that there continues to be a highly significant relationship (X^2 = 22.65, 2 d.f., p. <.001, C=.41) between marital status and social functioning, and that social class does not account for the difference in functioning between families headed by married couples and those headed by an unmarried mother. Only 3.6% of the families with unmarried mothers as against 53.5% of the other families were rated in the Adequate categories. Conversely, 50% of the unmarried mothers but only 19.8% of the others were rated as Problem Disposed (Problematic and Near Problematic), a classification that reflected difficulties not only in the instrumental area--these tended to be shared by most lower-class respondents--but in relationships to parents, relatives, boy friends, and putative fathers.

Family Functioning and Race

Approximately one-third of the sample families was Negro; the balance was white except for some 3% classified as other, which included Puerto Ricans[24] and some racially mixed marriages. Forty-six percent of Newark sample families as against 17% of New Brunswick and 31% of Plainfield families were Negro. Because of the sampling procedures these percentages reflect the proportion of Negroes in the universe specified in this study. However, the percentage of Negro families in the sample is higher than the proportion of Negroes in the 1960 population of the three cities.[25] The differences are probably a function of the larger ratio of Negroes to white among young families with a first child, but they may also reflect population changes which have taken place since the 1960 census.[26]

The social functioning of young Negro families was found to be significantly more problematic than that of the white families. (X^2 = 29.81, 2 d.f., p< .001, C = .35). This relationship is in line with a widely held view on the nature of the Negro family, a view which was strengthened by the much discussed and controversial Moynihan Report. Elizabeth Herzog on the other hand, when discussing the question of breakdown of the Negro family, criticized gross comparisons which do not take into account the socio-economic differentials between Negroes and whites.

> Adequately controlled comparisons within different income levels show that the differences associated with income outweigh those associated with color. Family structure, for example, differs more between different income levels than between Negro and white families. The same is true of differences between Negro and white children in educational achievement, and--when income is controlled--the relative position of men with respect to women, economically and educationally, is the same for whites as for nonwhites.[27]

Herzog's argument would lead us to hypothesize that differences in family functioning between Negroes and whites, such as those stated above, are primarily the result of differences in social stratification. It would then follow that holding the class factor constant in a comparison of social functioning would cause the differences between the racial groups to disappear.

This is essentially what happens when comparisons
are made separately for three status groups. Combining
classes I to IV of the revised Hollingshead Scale,[28] we find
no significant association (X^2 = .38, 1 d.f., p < .70) between
race and family functioning. The same is substantially true
for Class V (X^2 = 1.38, 1 d.f., p < .30) and Class VI (X^2 =
2.00, 1.d.f., p < .20). Thus the conclusion emerges that
differences in the nature of family functioning between Negroes and whites are spurious and can be seen largely as a
function of social class, not race.[29]

Social Functioning of Family of Procreation and
Families of Orientation

It has been argued in the social work literature that
problematic behavior tends to be socially inherited[30] and
that multi-problem functioning, in particular, is handed down
from generation to generation.[31] The present study offered
an opportunity to investigate this hypothesis, to test whether
the functioning of the young family or family of procreation,
is correlated with that of their families of orientation.[32]
The interview with the young mothers included a series of
questions on the social functioning of the two families of orientation, questions paralleling those asked about the family
of procreation. The respondent was asked to describe the
psycho-social situation of the parental homes in the recent
past. The information which was received was not nearly
so detailed as that pertaining to family of procreation, the
major gaps occurring in the data on the husband's family of
orientation. In out-of-wedlock situations, where the putative
father was absent, questions about his family of orientation
were not appropriate; in a few other cases the wife simply
did not have enough information to make reporting feasible.

Since the information on the functioning of families of
orientation lacked specificity, it seemed advisable to dichoto-
mize the data into Adequate and Less-than-Adequate categories, thus combining Near Adequate, Near Problematic,
and Problematic functioning. The results of cross-tabulating
the functioning of the families of procreation and orientation
are shown in Table 8.

A strongly significant relationship was discovered between the social functioning of the families of procreation

Table 8

Relationship in Social Functioning Between
Family of Procreation and Families of Orientation

Social Functioning of Family of Procreation	Social Functioning of Woman's Family of Orientation		Social Functioning of Man's Family of Orientation	
	Percent of Families			
	Adequate	Less Than Adequate	Adequate	Less Than Adequate
Adequate	70. 7	35. 4	72. 5	39. 5
Less than Adequate	29. 3	64. 6	27. 5	60. 5
Total Percent	100. 0	100. 0	100. 0	100. 0
N's	99	96	91	76

and that of the mother's families of orientation on the one hand (X^2 = 24. 56, 1 d. f. , p < . 001, C = . 32) and that of the father's families of orientation, on the other (X^2 = 18. 50, 1 d. f. , p < . 001, C = . 31). In approximately two-thirds of the sample cases similarity of functioning between the two generations is indicated by the data in Table 8. However, slightly more than one-third of the individuals whose families of orientation were in the Less than Adequate category now head families considered Adequate. Conversely, somewhat fewer than one-third of the young people coming from Adequate homes are rated in the Less than Adequate category. These sets of figures could be interpreted as a tendency on the part of the young families to function only slightly better than their respective families of orientation. [33]

The need for caution when interpreting these findings must be emphasized. In the first place, the categorization into Adequate and Less than Adequate is crude and may obscure inter-generational differences which remained hidden in the analysis. Secondly, the two groups of families, which were compared, stood at different points in the family life cycle. Exploring the influence of life-cycle stage upon family functioning remains one of the goals of the continuing research of which this study is only a part. With caution, therefore, we may state that the present analysis suggests a high degree of similarity and continuity rather than change in the social functioning of the two generations of families studied.

Continuity from family of orientation to family of procreation is also expressed by significant associations between the social class of the young families and that of the woman's family (X^2 = 22.32, 1 d.f., p <.001, C = .34) and of the man's family of orientation (X^2 = 16.54, 1 d.f., p <.001, C = .35).[34] Shifts in status from family of orientation to family of procreation were in both directions, with the younger generation showing a slight but statistically nonsignificant tendency toward more upward than downward mobility. That is somewhat surprising since middle-aged families have usually acquired a higher social position than younger families. In the population studied the slight upward mobility reflects the extension of the young husbands' formal education, since many of these young people had parents who grew up in rural environments and lacked the educational opportunities of the city.

To assess the relative effect of class upon the relationship between the functioning of family of procreation and that of the families of orientation, we correlated the latter two variables but held class constant. Even with class controlled, the cross-tabulation results showed that there continues to be a statistically significant association between the family functioning of the two generations (for the woman's family: Higher Class - X^2 = 5.57, C = .24, Lower Class - X^2 = 9.56, C = .29; for the man's family: Higher Class - X^2 = 4.97, C = .23; Lower Class - X^2 = 6.70, C = .28; 1 d.f. on all tables; all chi squares are significant at 5% level or better). It appears that the quality of family life in the parental home is a major factor determining the nature of functioning in the family founded by the young couple.

Other Factors Related to Family Functioning

A number of other variables, related to the young couple's pre-marital and early marital experience, were examined to determine their relationship to family functioning. The length of time the couple was acquainted before marriage was not significantly related, but length of engagement showed a very significant, positive association with the social functioning of the family (X^2 = 22.48, 1 d.f., p < .001 C = .34).   The duration of the engagement was also significantly associated with social status (X^2 = 20.51, 1 d.f., p < .001, C = .33).   When class was held constant the length of the engagement period continued to show a significant relationship to family functioning (for the Higher Class X^2 = 4.44, 1 d.f., p < .05; for the Lower Class - X^2 = 14.08, 1 d.f., p < .001).   In other words the correlation between longer engagements and social functioning cannot be seen as a function of class status.

The marriage age of both the father and the mother was directly related to level of functioning (X^2 = 7.64, 1 d.f., p < .01; X^2 = 4.82, 1 d.f., p < .05), which is to say that those who married young were less likely to be the head of a well functioning family than those who married when they were older.   Here again, social class was correlated with age at marriage for both the father (X^2 = 8.06, 1 d.f., p < .01) and mother (X^2 = 8.60, 1 d.f., p < .01).   However, when we control for class, the original relationship between age at marriage and family functioning disappears.   In short, this association is spurious and the result of class differences at marriage age.

The use of birth control was found to be unrelated to either social class or family functioning, but mothers who stated that the baby was planned headed families which functioned better than mothers who admitted to lack of planning (X^2 = 4.54, 1 d.f., p < .05, C = .15).   Planning of the child was more strongly and significantly related to social class (X^2 = 12.41, 1 d.f., p < .001, C = .24), with the higher classes more likely to have planned the baby.   The positive relationship between family planning and family functioning disappeared when class was held constant.

Whether the family heads were born in the sample city or state, or moved to it later appeared unrelated to the social functioning of the family of procreation. [35]   Data on other aspects, such as time of migration and length of time spent in differing urban or rural locations, were not coded.

The woman's current evaluation of the marriage (where there was a marriage) was very significantly related to the researcher's ratings of family functioning level (X^2 = 14.78, 1 d.f., p < .001, C = .30).   Social class per se showed a low, direct, but statistically non-significant relationship to the woman's positive evaluation of the marriage.

Some Attitudinal Correlates of Family Functioning

This study inquired into the mother's attitudes on social integration, marital relationship, and child socialization
because of an implicit hypothesis that such attitudes are related to family functioning. Catherine S. Chilman, in analyzing the literature on child rearing, shows that behavior patterns and attitudes characteristic of the very poor tend to
diverge sharply from those usually identified as conducive to
emotional health and positive socialization. [36]

Parental attitudes, which may be viewed as predisposi-
tions toward action in child rearing, naturally assume great
importance in a project which addresses itself to the issue of
prevention.

The question raised in this research can be stated as
follows: Are there identifiable attitudes in the areas of social integration and marital and parent-child relationships
which are associated with family malfunctioning? As an index to such attitudes we utilized the Srole Anomie Scale[37]
and ten scales of the PARI or Parental Attitude Research Instrument. [38] In each sample family the mother completed the
Srole and PARI scales in the presence of the research interviewer. Each scale is composed of five statements, cover-
ing the same area of content and calling for one of four possible responses to each item: strongly agree, agree, disagree, strongly disagree. Respondents were given a choice
of reading the schedule and checking the answers themselves
or having the statements read and the answers checked by the
interviewer. Under the latter arrangement the interviewee
was given the option of following the words of the interviewer
by reading the schedule.

A high score, indicating high agreement, on the Anomie
Scale signifies a rejection of community norms and is generally interpreted as non-integration in, and alienation from society. These high scores imply attitudes on family relations
and child rearing which are widely regarded as inimical to
emotional health and child socialization. [39]

The ten PARI scales are listed below and are more
fully identified as to content where necessary.

Fostering Dependency (children should be sheltered
from difficulties) Breaking the Will (children

must learn early who is boss) Martyrdom
(mothers sacrifice much for their children) Excluding Outside Influences (critical of parental behavior) Avoidance of Communication (about
troublesome subjects) Inconsiderateness of Husband (husbands tend to be unkind) Suppression of
Sexuality (keep sex from the child) Ascendance of
the Mother (mother bears the major responsibility)
Intrusiveness (a child must have no secrets) Acceleration of Development (children should be
pushed in their development)

The findings from the present analysis are briefly
summarized below.

An anomic attitude on the part of the mothers was
found to be significantly related to family malfunctioning
(X^2 = 9. 62, 1 d. f. , p < .01, C = . 21).   Anomie was similarly or slightly more strongly associated with social class
(X^2 = 12. 25, 1 d. f. , p < .001, C = . 24).   When the association between anomie and family functioning was tested but
class was held constant, the significant correlation between
the independent and dependent variables disappeared for the
higher classes and was reduced to a low magnitude which
did not reach 5% for the lower classes.   Hence it may be
concluded that family functioning and an anomic attitude do
not interact significantly independent of the families' social
class.

As a corollary the analysis established a significant
association between race and anomie, with the Negro mothers
showing more extreme attitudes of alienation than the white
mothers in the sample population (X^2 = 17. 42, 1 d. f. , p
< .001, C = . 28).   Even when class was controlled we found
a continuing association at the 5% level between race and
anomie in both higher and lower status groups.   Clearly, the
Negro mother's greater alienation cannot be accounted for by
her predominatly lower-class position.

Residence, too, showed an association with anomie of
the mother, with Newark mothers tending to be more alien-
ated than the residents of the two smaller communities, New
Brunswick and Plainfield (X^2 = 8. 60, 1 d. f. , p < .01, C = . 20).
Controlling for class, however, led to the elimination of this
correlation in the higher status category.   For lower class
mothers, those living in Newark still indicated a greater
feeling of alienation than those living in the smaller cities

$(X^2 = 8.50, 1 \text{ d.f.}, p < .01, C = .26)$.

Attitudes expressed through the PARI scales are viewed here as tendencies on the part of the respondent to act in ways which are either conducive to emotional health and child socialization (low scores) or harmful to both (high scores). For purposes of the present paper we accept this as an assumption that has some support in the child development literature[40] without discussing in detail the significance of each individual scale. Table 9 shows the relationship of the 10 PARI scales to family functioning.

Table 9

Relationship Between 10 PARI Scales
and Family Functioning

Name of Scale	X^2*	P	C (contingency coefficient)
Fostering Dependency	4.81	.05	.15
Breaking the Will	1.05	not significant**	.07
Martyrdom	1.82	not significant**	.09
Excluding Outside Influences	12.48	< .001	.24
Avoidance of Communication	11.23	< .001	.22
Inconsiderateness of Husband	5.15	< .05	.15
Suppression of Sexuality	10.72	< .01	.22
Ascendance of Mother	13.40	< .001	.24
Intrusiveness	9.56	< .01	.21
Acceleration of Develop't	16.95	< .001	.28

* Degree of freedom is 1 on all cross tabulations.
** p is below the 5% level of significance.

Inspection of Table 9 makes it clear that all but two scales, Breaking the Will (of the child) and Martyrdom (of the mother), are significantly correlated with family functioning. The association is in one direction only: Mothers showing less adequate functioning tend to score high or respond affirmatively to the statements in the PARI scales. The correlation is most pronounced on Acceleration of Development where mothers of less adequately functioning families seem to express a desire to push the children ahead in their development.

The same ten scales are also correlated with social class of the family, with the lower-class mothers showing attitudes generally identified as less conducive to good socialization and to the mental health of the child.

The correlation between attitudes and class is statistically highly significant on all the dimensions, and the likelihood of its being a chance association can be rejected at the 1% level for the two scales Fostering Dependency and Breaking the Will and at the .1% level or better for the remaining eight scales. Class thus emerges as a major factor influencing mothers' views on child rearing and family relationships.

To what extent, it may be asked, is the relationship between high scoring on the PARI and family malfunctioning merely a function of social class, which, it will be recalled, is also significantly related to social functioning of the family? The answer is given in Table 10.

Table 10

Relationship Between 10 PARI Scales and Family Functioning With Class Held Constant

Name of Scale	x^2 for * Higher Class	p	x^2 for Lower Class	p
Fostering Dependency	0.00	not sig. **	1.13	not sig.
Breaking the Will	0.02	"	0.24	"
Martyrdom	0.82	"	0.45	"
Excluding Outside Influence	0.18	"	6.32	< .02
Avoidance of Communication	0.01	"	6.97	< .01
Inconsiderateness of Husband	0.19	"	3.45	not sig.
Suppression of Sexuality	0.17	"	5.59	< .02
Ascendance of Mother	2.86	"	2.81	not sig.
Intrusiveness	0.06	"	1.44	not sig.
Acceleration of Development	0.66	"	9.60	< .01

* Degree of freedom is 1 on all cross tabulations.
** At at least the 5% level.

Controlling for class, Table 10 shows us that most of
the attitudes tapped in the PARI scales are no longer significantly related to family functioning.   For the higher status group, associations between the two variables are of a
low magnitude and largely due to chance.   Similarly, the relationship between parental attitudes and family functioning
in the lower status group is not statistically significant, with
the exception of the four scales called Excluding Outside Influence, Avoidance of Communication, Suppression of Sexuality, and Acceleration of Development.   Therefore, the original association between parental attitudes and family functioning can be held to be chiefly a function of social status, although in some attitude areas lower-class mothers tend to
function more adequately when they come   close to the so-
called desirable views on child rearing and family relationships.

Summary of Findings on the Correlates
of Problem Functioning

In summarizing the data on the correlates of problem
functioning we observe, first of all, that family malfunctioning is clearly linked to social class.   Lower status families
are much more likely to be problem disposed than higher
status families.   Marital status is a further significant factor in social malfunctioning, with families headed by unmarried mothers functioning more poorly than two-parent families.   The functioning of the maternal and paternal families
of orientation emerges as a highly significant variable influencing the functioning of the young family of procreation, regardless of their social status.   Length of engagement appears to be a prognostic factor in marriage, with longer engagement periods associated with more adequate social functioning, regardless of class position of the couple.   The
woman's positive evaluation of the current marital situation
was found to be significantly associated with the level of
family functioning as assessed by the researcher.

Attitudes of alienation from society were found to be
more characteristic of lower-class living than of problematic
family functioning.   Attitudes on child rearing and family relations, likewise, were more classbound than tied to the level of social functioning.   Yet, several attitude dimensions
in the area of child rearing did appear correlated with social functioning, at least in the lower-status population.
Mothers who endorsed statements on the Exclusion of Outside

Influences, Avoidance of Communication, Suppression of
Sexuality, and Acceleration of Development were more likely
to be at the head of problematic families.

As it is the objective of this study to sketch the beginning outlines of a model for professional intervention in
family malfunctioning, the above analysis is seen as relevant in two respects: It can help in identifying the problem-
prone families by considering the correlates of family malfunctioning; it can provide a springboard for a causative exploration and appropriately focused treatment in the social
functioning of the family. Both processes would appear to
be important prerequisites to that kind of service planning
which puts a premium on prevention rather than on remedial
intervention.

As a next step we shall consider some research alternatives for constructing models of early intervention such
that it offers a potential for prevention.

Notes

1.   The interviews were conducted for the most part by
      students of the Rutgers Graduate School of Social
      Work. Up to five attempts were made to locate a
      family in their home.

2.   Comparable data were not available from Plainfield
      and New Brunswick.

3.   Family Life Improvement Project, "Progress Report,
      February, 1966" Graduate School of Social Work,
      Rutgers-the State University, New Brunswick, N. J.
      (Mimeographed.)

4.   Sample attrition as was shown above is largely a
      function of family mobility. Such mobility appears to
      be extremely high at the early stage of the family
      life cycle. While the Newark data showed that within
      a year of the time the births were reported about 40%
      of the families could not be found living at the ad-
      dress listed, the percentages for cases which could
      not be located rose to 60% in the second and 75% in
      the third year.

5.   Earl S. Schaefer and Richard A. Bell, "Development

of a Parental Attitude Research Instrument," Child
Development, Vol. XXIX, No. 3, Sept. 1938, pp.
339-361.

6. Leo Srole, "Social Integration and Certain Corollaries: An Exploratory Study," American Sociological Review, Vol. XXI, No. 6, Dec., 1956, pp. 709-
716.

7. Includes Puerto Ricans, although this group was
under-represented because the research project had
few Spanish-speaking interviewers.

8. For evidence in support of this assumption see National Association of Social Workers, Research Interviewing in Sensitive Areas. New York, National Association of Social Workers, 1963.

9. Gordon E. Brown (editor). The Multi-Problem
Dilemma, Metuchen, N. J., The Scarecrow Press,
Inc. 1968. pp. 107-181.

See David Wallace, "The Chemung County Evaluation
of Casework Services to Dependent Multi-Problem
Families," The Social Service Review, op. cit.

10. Work now in progress at the Rutgers Social Work Research Center has as its goal the conceptual refinement of the category Adequate functioning. This effort will hopefully lead to a more normal distribution
of the variables in family functioning even among young
families.

11. The areas, eight in number are: Family Relationships and Unity, Individual Behavior and Adjustment,
Care and Training of Children, Social Activities,
Economic Practices, Household Practices, Health
Conditions and Practices, Use of Community Resources. A ninth area used in the St. Paul Scale,
Relationship to Social Worker, is not employed here
because few families in the research sample maintained any contact with social workers.

12. A more detailed account of the Profiles of Family
Functioning for the Near Adequate, Near Problematic,
and Problematic groups is shown in Table 2.

13.   For a more precise definition see Geismar and
        LaSorte, op. cit. , pp. 31-43 and 215-222.

14.   The chief evidence for this hypothesis is the New
        Brunswick cross-sectional study of two random
        samples of families cited below.   Other converging
        evidence is found in studies of older families known
        to agencies which investigated problems of economic
        dependency or behavior problems of the child.
        These families revealed a substantially more prob-
        lematic profile than the families in this study.   See
        Geismar, "Family Functioning as an Index for Need
        of Welfare Services," loc. cit.

15.   This is a smaller ratio than the estimates for two
        medium sized North American cities.   See Geismar
        and LaSorte, op. cit. , pp. 57-64.

16.   The percentages exceed one hundred because most
        mothers cited more than one family goal.

17.   The small number professing this goal should not be
        seen as evidence that happiness is not a family goal.
        In fact over half of the study group indicated during
        the course of the interview that the marriage meets
        or exceeds their positive expectations.   The above
        response would suggest that most families considered
        a happy home life either a fact (not a goal) or a goal
        which was taken for granted and did not need articu-
        lation.

18.   Although the literature in support of this thesis is
        much too large to be cited, the following examples
        might be mentioned: Lola M. Irelan, "Health Prac-
        tices of the Poor," Welfare in Review, Vol. III, No.
        10, Oct. , 1965, pp. 1-9.   M. Allen Pond, "Poverty
        and Disease," Social Welfare Forum 1961.   New
        York, Columbia University Press, 1961, pp. 59-72.
        August B. Hollingshead and Frederick C. Redlich,
        Social Class and Mental Illness: A Community Study.
        New York, John Wiley and Sons, Inc. , 1958.   Roland
        T. Chilton, "Continuity in Delinquency Area Re-
        search: A Comparison of Studies for Baltimore, De-
        troit and Indianapolis," American Sociological Review,
        Vol. XXIX, No. 1. Feb. , 1964, pp. 71-83.

19.   Hollingshead and Redlich, op. cit.

20.   The terms class, status, and social position are
       used here interchangeably.

21.   Based upon a reanalysis of the New Haven Data by
       Professor William D. Wells of Rutgers University.

22.   Newark families were selected randomly from the
       total number of first births which occurred during
       the first eight months of 1962. New Brunswick and
       Plainfield families, by contrast, represent all the
       first births during the same time span in 1963. Sta-
       tistical inference on the latter group of cases can be
       justified by arguing that families who gave birth to a
       first child during the first months of 1963 do not dif-
       fer from families who had their first child before or
       after that period. In other words, our statistical in-
       ference in the case of the small city families is
       made from the sample to the universe of first births
       during the early 1960's in the particular communities.

23.   Social status data on five of the sample of 39 un-
       married mothers were insufficient to establish status
       classification.

24.   Puerto Ricans were underrepresented since a number
       of interviews could not be conducted because of the
       language barrier.

25.   The 1960 census lists the following percentages of
       Negroes relative to total population: Newark 34%,
       New Brunswick 15%, Plainfield 22%. Source: U. S.
       Bureau of Census. U. S. Census of Population and
       Housing: 1960. Census tracts. Final Report PHC
       (1)-105. Washington, D. C., U. S. Govt. Prtg. Office,
       1962.

26.   A Rutgers University population and labor force sur-
       vey estimated the percentage of Negroes in Newark
       in the Spring of 1967 as 52. Jack Chernick, Bernard
       P. Indik, and George Sternlieb, Newark-New Jersey
       Population and Labor Force. New Brunswick, N. J.,
       Rutgers-The State University, December, 1967, p. 3.

27.   Elizabeth Herzog, "Is There a Breakdown in the
       Negro Family?" Social Work, Vol. II, No. 1, Janu-
       ary, 1966, pp. 3-10, p. 7.

28.   There were no Negroes in Class I, two in Class II,
        four in Class III, and five in Class IV, making a
        total of eleven in classes I to IV.

29.   A later study, using families served by the Rutgers
        Family Life Improvement Project, emerged with sub-
        stantially similar results except for findings on Class
        V families, which revealed statistically significant
        differences in social functioning between Negroes and
        whites. For the study and attempts at explaining
        this partial inconsistency see Ludwig L. Geismar and
        Ursula C. Gerhart, "Social Class, Ethnicity, and
        Family Functioning: Exploring Some Issues Raised
        by the Moynihan Report," Journal of Marriage and the
        Family, Vol. XXX, No. 3, August, 1968, pp. 480-
        487.

30.   Bradley Buell and Associates, Community Planning
        for Human Services. New York, Columbia Univer-
        sity Press, 1952, p. 260ff.

31.   L. L. Geismar, "The Multi-Problem Family: Signifi-
        cance of Research Findings," The Social Welfare
        Forum 1960. New York, Columbia University Press,
        1960.

32.   Particularly relevant are the findings of a number of
        investigators showing a direct relationship between
        marital adjustment of couples and the happiness of
        their parents' marriage. See Clifford Kirkpatrick,
        "Measuring Marital Adjustment," Selected Studies in
        Marriage and the Family, ed. Robert Winch, Robert
        McGinnis, and Herbert R. Barringer. New York,
        Holt, Rinehart and Winston, 1962, pp. 544-553.

33.   This finding is not necessarily in contradiction to the
        basic research hypothesis which postulates increasing
        family malfunctioning from the very early to subse-
        quent life cycle stages, particularly the middle stages.
        It is quite probable, and there is some beginning em-
        pirical evidence supporting the notion, that older fami-
        lies, which survive the child launching stage, func-
        tion more adequately than middle stage ones and
        nearly as well as younger ones. See Geismar and
        LaSorte, op. cit., pp. 169-170.

34.   The small chi square for the relationship between

family of procreation and the man's family of
orientation is the result of the small N (reflecting
missing information) on the cross tabulation.

35.   Negro fathers and mothers were more likely to
       have come from out of state than were white family
       heads, but the difference was not statistically signifi-
       cant.

36.   Catherine S. Chilman, "Child Rearing and Family Re-
       lationship Patterns of the Very Poor," Welfare in
       Review, Vol. III, no. 1, Jan., 1965, pp. 9-19.

37.   Leo Srole, "Social Integration and Certain Corollaries:
       An Exploratory Study," American Sociological Re-
       view, Vol. XXI, No. 6, Dec., 1956, pp. 709-716.

38.   Earl S. Schaefer and Richard A. Bell, "Development
       of a Parental Attitude Research Instrument," Child
       Development, Vol. XXVIII, No. 3, Sept., 1958, pp.
       339-316.   The ten most reliable of the 23 PARI
       scales, appropriate to the present research, were
       used in this study.

39.   For evidence in support of this thesis see Ibid, pp.
       10-13.   It must be stressed, however, that we are
       dealing in this study only with mothers' attitudes
       and that little has been done to relate these to ob-
       served behavior.   The authors of the PARI them-
       selves have counseled potential users to use the
       scales only as an economical first approach in un-
       charted areas.   See Wesley C. Becker and Ronald
       S. Krug, "The Parent Attitude Research Instrument -
       A Research Review," Child Development, Vol.
       XXXVI, No. 2, June, 1965, pp. 330-365, p. 359.

40.   Chilman, loc. cit, pp. 10-14.

Chapter 3
Research Alternatives for Constructing
Models for Preventive Intervention

Planning a program of preventive intervention requires some basis for predicting the nature of malfunctioning that is likely to occur in the future. Utilizing the empirical approach, there are at least two methods that can be used to collect relevant data: (1) Actual family development or change over time can be studied by means of longitudinal or quasi-longitudinal techniques; (2) present family functioning can be used to forecast future malfunctioning. The foregoing data on the 216 young families provides the information base when the second alternative is used in this chapter. When the first approach is discussed, additional data of an empirical nature will be introduced, allowing an actual juxtaposition of family functioning at two life-cycle stages. We shall begin with the first method and, by introducing the additional research data, supply information that is relevant to the second approach.

(1) Developmental Studies of the Family as a Basis for Projecting Need for Intervention.

This study's group profile on the social functioning of young families does not yield information on the process of moving from a well functioning to a malfunctioning stage. The social functioning characteristics of the seriously disorganized family are fairly well known, [1] as are those of the socially adequate family, but the latter does not, save for exceptional cases, move toward utter malfunctioning. Where this happens the process is of long duration and the family will have passed through successive stages of problematic functioning less severe than the state of serious disorganization.

Since presumably less than 5% of urban families are truly multi-problem or disorganized, [2] the bulk of families in any randomly selected urban sample are likely to experience problematic functioning of a lesser magnitude. What

is the nature of this malfunctioning? Stated within the context of our design to prevent malfunctioning among young
families the question can be posed as follows: What is the
dynamic change pattern in social functioning for a cross section of young urban families?

The Rutgers Family Life Improvement Project, as
stated earlier, is studying young families longitudinally in
order to answer the foregoing question. At present some
guidance on the issue comes from two sources: (1) A comparison of social functioning patterns of the 216 families in
the present study with those of two groups of older agency
clients, one composed of recipients of Aid to Families with
Dependent Children and the other made up of families receiving treatment revolving around the behavior problems of
a child.[3] Neither group could be termed socially disorganized. (2) The second study is a comparison of the social functioning of a selected sample of families having children in
middle school with a random sample of young families having a first child below the age of one, both family groups
residing in New Brunswick, New Jersey.[4]

The family functioning profiles of the agency clients,
who as a group are characterized by substantial social adequacy, reveal problems mainly in the intra- and interpersonal areas of behavior. In this respect they show more
problematic functioning than the random sample of young
families. Deficiencies in social functioning are pronounced
in marital and parent-child relationships and in individual
behavior. Social activities, though not problematic by and
large, appear to be devoid of satisfaction. For lower-class
families in the agency samples, instrumental patterns of behavior such as economic, health, and household practices
leave much to be desired. In general, however, the agency
samples showed greater adequacy in their management of instrumental tasks than in their interpersonal relationships.
Although the two samples of families are characterized by
special needs, for which they received services, rather than
pervasive problematic behavior, we do not know whether
families with agency contacts of the kind reported here (the
cases receiving child hygiene services were predominantly
of middle-class background) are representative of the total
population with regard to their social functioning. Collective-
ly, their level of family functioning is considerably lower
than that of the young families studied.

A comparison of two family samples half a generation apart in age and chosen by random selection provides a better lead on the dynamic nature of family malfunctioning during the early part of the family life cycle.

Table 11 shows a comparison of younger and older families by means of percentages of cases in each age group who were rated as functioning at an Adequate, Near Adequate, and Problem Disposed level. The greater social adequacy of younger families is revealed in the percentage distribution and the statistical significance of the difference in family functioning between the two groups (X^2 = 9.47, 2 d.f., p <.01). The total social functioning scores do not disclose any of the qualitative aspects of family functioning for the two groups that are being compared. A comparative picture of the nature of family behavior for younger and older families becomes manifest by viewing the percentages of cases which function at an Adequate level by area of family functioning. This is shown in Table 12.

Table 11

The Social Functioning of Younger and
Older Families Compared

Level of Overall Social Functioning	Younger Families* %	N	Older Families %	N	Total N
Adequate	59.0	36	35.4	23	59
Near Adequate	27.9	17	27.7	18	35
Problem Disposed**	13.1	8	36.9	24	32
Total	100.0	61	100.0	65	126

* This is the same group of New Brunswick families that were used in an earlier section of this study. The two percent difference in the categorization of family functioning (see Table 4) is the result of a new rating done by a different group of raters. In order to provide maximum standardization in rating with the older families the new team of coders who had evaluated the older families supplied a new rating of the younger ones.

** Combines the categories Near Problematic and Problematic.

Table 12

Comparison of Younger and Older
Families by Area of Social Functioning

Areas of Family Functioning	Percent of Families Functioning Adequately		
	Younger Families	Older Families	Percentage Difference
	N=61	N=65	
Family Relationships and Unity	80. 3	69. 0	11. 3
Individual Behavior and Adjustment	80. 3	64. 6	15. 7
Care and Training of Children	90. 2	69. 2	21. 0
Social Activities	83. 6	67. 7	15. 9
Economic Practices	88. 5	56. 9	31. 6
Home & Household Practices	88. 5	53. 8	34. 7
Health Practices	96. 7	78. 5	18. 2
Use of Community Resources	96. 7	83. 1	13. 6

Although the percentage ratings on the areas of functioning do not indicate the level of functioning of families rated as less than Adequate--a refinement not warranted since most cases showing lesser adequacy are clustered in the Near Adequate category--they do provide us with a picture of differences between the two age-cohorts in the prevalence of social functioning which falls somewhat short of meeting basic family needs and community expectations.

The finding of lesser adequacy in overall family functioning in the older families is paralleled in every area of functioning. The trend is consistently in the direction of greater prevalence of malfunctioning in the families with school-aged children. The differential between the two groups is greatest in Home and Household Practices and Economic Practices, indicating that the older families encountered more problems in earning a living and in housing.

     The relatively greater difference between the two age-
cohorts in these two instrumental areas raises the question
of whether our random sampling techniques may have failed
to yield two populations with a similar socio-economic distribution.   A comparison in Table 13 of socio-economic ratings of
older and younger New Brunswick families shows this supposition to be correct.

Table 13

Socio-economic Status of Younger
and Older Families Compared

Social Class*	Percent of Younger Families	Percent of Older Families
	N=61	N=65
Class I - IV	45. 9	26. 1
Class V	36. 1	38. 5
Class VI	18. 0	35. 4
Total	100. 0	100. 0

* For an explanation see page 36

     Another question arises from the unanticipated and
rather striking differences in status distribution found between
the young and older families. [5]   Bearing in mind that our
earlier findings showed an association between functioning
and class, the question is whether present family functioning
is the result of social class differences.   Table 14 shows
that when class is controlled, younger families continue to
show more adequate functioning than older families.   However, with the N's now radically reduced, only the differences
for Class V and VI are clearly statistically significant
(Class V: X^2 = 4. 82, 1 d. f. , p < . 05; Class VI Fisher Exact
Test: 1 d. f. , p = . 007; Class I - IV: p is not significant.

     Having established that family life-cycle stage is a
probable factor influencing the nature of family functioning,
we can now look more analytically at the relationship between
family functioning and life-cycle stage by comparing areas of
social functioning while holding class constant.   This is done

Table 14

The Social Functioning of Older and Younger
Families Compared, with Class Held Constant

| Index of Social Status | Percent of Families Functioning Adequately | | |
	Younger Families N=61	Older Families N=65	Total N
Class I - IV	75.0	70.6	45
Class V	50.0	16.0	47
Class VI	36.3	0.0	34
			126

in Table 15, which shows that differences in adequacy of
family functioning are, with two exceptions, in favor of the
younger families. The two exceptions showing a reverse
direction are among the three smallest differences noted
(1.3% and 3.8%). There is a progressive decline in the extent of adequacy in each age cohort from one status group
to the next, but the decline is greater between Class I - IV
and V than between Class V and VI. Moreover, the inter-
class differences are somewhat greater for the older families (18.3% and 7.2%) than the younger ones (11.0% and
3.5%). Inter-cohort differences in each class increase as
social status declines, and the mean of these differences
exceeds in magnitude the inter-class differences for each cohort between Class V and VI. However, the inter-class gap
in mean level of adequacy between Class I - IV and Class V
is larger than the inter-cohort differences in both of these
classes.

At this point the data lend themselves to a first gen-
eralization. The stage of the family life cycle appears to
affect family functioning somewhat more greatly than does
the social class; however, the relative influence of social
class exceeds that of life-cycle stage at the upper end (between Class I - IV and V) of the status scale. At the lower
end (between Class V and VI) family age has relatively more
importance in determining the degree of adequacy in family
functioning. Therefore, if we view age cohort differences
in terms of class, we may conclude that the lower the social

Table 15

Differences Between Young and Old Families in the Percentages of
Cases Rated as Functioning Adequately by Social Class

Percent of Cases and Differences Between the
Percentage of Young and Old Families
Rated as Functioning Adequately

AREA OF FAMILY FUNCTIONING	CLASS I-IV			CLASS V			CLASS VI		
	Younger Families	Older Families	Difference	Younger Families	Older Families	Difference	Younger Families	Older Families	Difference
Family Relationships and Unity	96.4	88.2	8.2	63.6	60.0	3.6	72.7	65.2	7.5
Individual Behavior and Adjustment	96.4	76.5	19.9	68.2	72.0	-3.8*	63.3	52.2	11.1
Care and Training of Children	96.4	88.2	8.2	86.4	76.0	10.4	81.8	69.6	12.2
Social Activities	85.7	70.6	15.1	81.8	68.0	13.8	81.8	69.6	12.2
Economic Practices	92.8	94.1	-1.3*	90.9	44.0	46.9	72.7	43.5	29.2
Home and Household Practices	92.8	82.3	10.5	90.9	48.0	42.9	72.7	39.1	33.6

	Younger Families	Older Families	Difference	Younger Families	Older Families	Difference	Younger Families	Older Families	Difference
Health Practices	100.0	94.1	5.9	95.4	88.0	7.4	100.00	56.5	43.5
Use of Community Resources	100.0	88.2	11.8	95.4	80.0	15.4	100.0	82.6	17.4
Mean of Eight Areas	95.1	85.3	9.8	84.1	67.0	17.1	80.6	59.8	20.8

* A minus sign indicates that differences between percentages are in the opposite direction of that hypothesized.

status the more important such differences become.   This finding suggests that in the early stages of the family life cycle the social functioning of lower-class families declines more rapidly than that of higher status families.

Further inspection of Table 15 reveals that differences in specific areas of functioning between younger and older families are not uniformly distributed between the classes.   In the top status group the decline in adequacy is greatest in Individual Behavior and Adjustment, and Social Activities.   In the low status groups Economic Practices, Home and Household Practices, and Health Problems and Practices are the three areas showing the greatest reduction in adequacy.   In Class VI the two age-cohorts differ most in Health Problems and Practices, but in Class V health does not prove to be a strongly differentiating area.

For the overall quantitative picture of the differences in social functioning between younger and older families, we must compare the inter-cohort shifts in functioning patterns in the total sample of study families with the shifts in the three status groups.   The comparison takes the form of a matrix (Table 16) showing the rank order correlations (rhos) among the total sample and status groups for area by area differences between the two age-cohorts.

Table 16

Rhos Among Social Classes for Differences by
Area in Family Functioning Between Two Age Cohorts

	Total N	Class I - IV	Class V	Class VI
Total N		-.26	+.62	+.68
Class I-IV			-.30	-.43
Class V				+.59

Table 16 shows that differences in adequacy, ranked by area, between the two age-cohorts for the total sample (see Table 12) are not uniformly reflected in the three status groups.   For the most part, the area pattern of dif-

ferences for the total study sample reflects Class V and VI
patterns--the classes which constitute the bulk of the sample.
These classes have patterns which substantially resemble
each other as indicated by the moderately high rhos.   Status
group I to IV diverges substantially from the lower status
groups as indicated by the low negative rhos and is consequently at variance with the total sample, whose pattern is
determined to a large extent by the lower classes.   In short,
older and younger families differ in the pattern of adequacy
in social functioning, and the nature of the differences varies
according to class.   In the highest status group the greatest
discrepancy in adequacy between age cohorts is in the areas
of behavior and social relationship, while in the low status
groups it lies in the instrumental areas of functioning.

The foregoing analysis suggests that we need to take
socio-economic status into account if we use existing differences between age-cohorts of families as a guide for
developing a prevention model.   It appears that as lower-
class families get older they experience relatively greater
pressures in instrumental areas, whereas families in the
higher social strata encounter proportionately more difficulties in behavior and social relationship areas.   This observation notwithstanding, it should be remembered that lower
status families, starting from a lower level of social functioning, experience a higher measure of overall decline than
higher status families.

The method of inferring change in social functioning
from studying cohorts of families at different life cycle
stages is at best an imperfect substitute for longitudinal research on the same population, for, as the reader will have
already discovered, it is exceedingly difficult to locate age
cohorts of families which are sociologically comparable.
The random sampling technique within the same community
seemed promising enough until it was discovered that two
randomly selected age cohorts differed substantially in socio-
economic composition.   We sought the reasons for this by
inferring from our knowledge about the geographic mobility
of families, so characteristic of the metropolis and apparently affecting suburban communities such as New Brunswick as
well.   The comparability of the two cohorts was improved
by controlling for social class but this still fell short of
supplying the researcher with truly analogous family groups
from which developmental changes in family functioning
could be deduced with confidence.   In spite of these shortcomings, the cross-sectional study method used here repre-

sents a first approximation to longitudinal research and permits data collection within a change perspective that is relevant to preventive planning.

(2) Analysis of Present Family Functioning as a Basis for
Projecting Need for Intervention

While longitudinal and cross-sectional analysis of
different age-cohorts represent promising approaches to the
study of prevention, they have inherent limitations, such as
cost, time required, and sampling problems.   These limitations make it mandatory to find techniques for projecting
family functioning change and designing models for preventive
intervention.   One such method is the analysis of present
patterns of family functioning, which can be viewed as useful
within the context of what Bross calls persistence prediction. [6]   This is one of several techniques used by the decision maker, which assumes that the present is a guide to
the future.   Bross states that the technique has limitations
and works only "in relatively stable or slowly changing situations,"[7] a condition which, we assume, applies to family
functioning.   Used in social functioning, persistence prediction means that a forecast about future malfunctioning can be
made from the existing pattern of functioning, to the extent
that emergent problematic functioning is an indication of
more serious problem functioning to come.   This assumption
may be considered valid if that which holds true for medicine, namely that limited pathology is likely to become major, has application to the field of human behavior.   Tentative evidence to support this thesis in the field of family behavior is contained in the finding that family functioning is
scalable. [8] or cumulative in a unidimensional direction.

Preventive planning that uses predictions derived from
a static situation as a point of departure, instead of knowledge about the truly dynamic character of social functioning,
will probably stress secondary rather than primary prevention, largely gearing itself to coping with identified emergent malfunctioning.   At the same time, primary prevention
can also be part of the overall intervention strategy.   Some
action planning will be focused on projected malfunctioning
which has not yet manifested itself.

What information does the social functioning profile
of the young family convey which can be the basis for planning preventive intervention?   Briefly summarized, the pro-

file reveals that the greatest problemicity will occur in
families of lower-class background, or which are headed by
unmarried mothers, or which are formed by the offspring
of families which manifested social malfunctioning. Families showing limited malfunctioning were most likely to have
problems in intra-familial relationships; those characterized
by more pervasive malfunctioning showed problems in family
relations, individual behavior and, to a lesser extent, in
instrumental areas. From a prediction perspective which
seeks to rely largely on present social functioning, malfunctioning can be read as vulnerability to more extensive
problem functioning in the future.

If the degree of problemicity is used as a predictor,
the areas of social relationships will become the major focal points of intervention in all family groups showing limited problemicity. By contrast, treatment focus on instrumental behavior is most likely to occur only in families
showing considerable problemicity in their overall social
functioning pattern.

When the spotlight is shifted and families are seen
in their socio-economic groupings, it becomes increasingly
clear that the balance between social relationships, particularly intra-familial ones, and instrumental functioning is related. In the highest socio-economic groups both spheres
of functioning reveal a similar degree of high adequacy.
In Class VI there is a comparable picture at the lower end
of the social adequacy scale. Class V, by contrast, is
characterized by a family profile which manifests more
widespread problematic functioning in family relationships
than in the economic, health, and housing areas. Planning
for prevention in the lowest social class, therefore, is more
likely to be of a two-pronged nature, seeking to cope with
weaknesses in economic areas and interpersonal relationships as well, while preventive intervention in the middle
status group is more likely to be concentrated on the latter
area. In the highest classes a cross-sectional, problem-
focused group profile may provide little help for those
planning preventive intervention. Instead, examination of
past family experiences and individual behavior for a specific family pattern might prove to be the better guide.
While individualized family diagnosis should never be disre-
garded in planning for prevention, it may loom relatively
larger in importance where the group picture is one of
basic adequacy.

It becomes clear from studying the social functioning
analyses of Tables 2 and 15, the first based on three levels
of adequacy or problemicity and the second on social status,
that generalizations about young families as a whole are of
limited validity. Striking differences among members of
the sub-groups are found in both tables, underscoring the
need to approach the subject of prevention within the context
of conceptually meaningful groupings. Degree of problemicity and socio-economic class are two such groupings, en-
abling us to view family behavior as differentiated, yet relatively homogeneous entities. But in using these two categories we have merely begun meaningful exploration of the
dynamics of family functioning. Other potentially promising
approaches are the analyses of families that have migrated
from rural areas, that have experienced downward or upward mobility following marriage, that have immigrated,
that are cohesive ethnic groups--and these do not exhaust
the list. Sociological groupings such as these which are
known to influence various aspects of human behavior may
be assumed to leave their mark on the trajectory of family
functioning.

Strategies of Early Intervention[9]

In addition to the data on 216 young and 65 older families, which were analyzed in the foregoing section, our proposed outline of a model for intervention will also incorpo-
rate information and insights from interviews not yet fully
processed, conducted with an additional 460 young Newark
families who are the test subjects for the Family Life Improvement Project.

Though it is beyond the scope of this paper to discuss specific techniques of intervention, there is need to
mention the key roles played by the worker as he offers services to the family. The respondents, when asked in the interview to whom they would turn when they face a serious
problem or experience a time of crisis, listed friends and
relatives, doctors, or clergymen. While these persons
might indeed be helpful, there is also a danger that their advice represents a lay viewpoint, narrowly focussed and perhaps colored by personal considerations. The social worker,
when aiding the family, establishes himself as a primary
community resource and a channel to other existing resources. As intervenor he provides information, guidance,
and advice by consulting with or bringing in professional

specialists; he acts as mediator and communications link between client and resource, and whenever possible he functions directly as counselor, enabler, and problem-solver.

Bringing community resources or even the knowledge
that these exist to the family may serve to prevent crisis
or breakdown in the future.   When using community resources, early intervention is likely to be most truly preventive if services rendered are directed toward coping with
possible, anticipated problem functioning rather than the
solution of existing problems.   The worker will seek to enhance the client's communication skill when dealing with the
community agencies and services which can serve as a resource for dealing with different kinds of problems.   Granted
that such resources in the American community are scarce
and generally underdeveloped, we nonetheless postulate that
non-use by potential clients is to no small measure the result of an absence of knowledge about them and a lack of social skill on the part of those families who deal with them.
If appropriate community facilities and services are indeed
absent, the intervention agency should whenever possible act
as the extra resource which in one form or another will
find the means to render assistance to the family either by
creating make-shift resources or stretching existing services
to cover the client.

The social worker engaged in preventive services who
attempts to bring deficient or poorly developed resources to
the family will find himself playing two somewhat non-tradi-
tional roles: that of the broker and the advocate. [10] As a
broker he will serve as an intermediary between client and
agency, seeking to bring about policy changes at the local
level for groups of clients such as those with which he is
dealing.   As an advocate he argues the client's point of view
with an eye toward modifying agency policy and/or practice.
In both roles the worker takes a partisan position, particularly pronounced when he acts the advocate who has, in fact,
decided that the client is not receiving his due.

Based on the foregoing presentation and analysis of
empirical data, we can proceed to propose several broad
modes of professional intervention.   In doing this our reference is to the knowledge we have gained about family functioning and about probable changes in these patterns as the
family grows older.   Suggested modes will take into account
the nature of the families' overall functioning and their
socio-economic status.

(a) Intervention programming appropriate to the level of Adequate or Near Adequate family functioning cannot look for much guidance from the limited data about social malfunctioning. Families in these categories are more likely to be from the higher socio-economic status groups, and such problems as they do enounter tend to be in the individual behavior and family relationship areas.

Adequate and Near Adequate families are usually able to recover from crises without intensive services. Consequently, appropriate intervention is likely to take the form of giving information and advice, steering toward resources offering limited counselling for behavior or relationship problems. Essentially, service at this level means building upon existing family strengths in order to help members overcome disappointment, anxiety, and frustration; it may also mean effecting some modification of environmental conditions to relieve stress. Education regarding the availability of resources in times of need, which we have discussed above, appears to be especially appropriate. On the whole, however, service here is on a stand-by basis, geared to respond with maximum flexibility to requests for help.

Preventive intervention with this group or any other group of families cannot limit itself, however, to action based on the actual or projected problem profile. Howard Parad, in a reference to the public health approach to prevention, states that "primary preventive activities refer to the promotion of an active state of positive health, which obviously involves promoting optimal life conditions at a preonset stage of problem or symptom development."[11] Family functioning, and malfunctioning for that matter, does not take place in a socio-cultural vacuum but occurs within the context of family hopes, aspirations, values, and life goals-- all of which circumscribe family behavior. The relationship between these goals and the family's actual opportunity to achieve them, may become an important determinant, albeit not the only one, of the character of family functioning. Thus preventive action must take cognizance of family values and aspirations and seek to encourage behavior which is in line with realistic goals. Prevention must do more than keep the family unit out of trouble and avoid problems. It must help the family arrive at an approach to life which permits the experience of satisfactions and the attainment of goals and aspirations.

The conditions for achieving both satisfaction and

goals are inherent in a family's psycho-social situation. That situation which comprises social, economic, biological, and psychological factors is not rigidly fixed but is in a state of flux as a result of the family's bio-social development and changes in the social structure. A program of prevention needs to address itself to the interplay of these forces within a perspective of family development. The intervenor, then, is more than a trouble shooter; he is an agent who helps the family identify and articulate life goals and examine alternate ways of attaining them.

We cannot, in the present analysis, even begin to identify life goals or to consider them relative to a family's social situation and achievement possibilities, but research on prevention will need ultimately to address itself fully to each one of these issues and their interrelationship. Nonetheless, under the present approach, viewing prevention within the context of social functioning, a design for action must give important consideration to the question of family goals. We venture the opinion that preventive intervention with a beginning focus on family values and aspirations is particularly important when working with Adequate and Near Adequate families. Lacking evidence of social malfunctioning or areas of concern in family life, the intervening agent requires a focus of action which is related to the family's normal development. Where problems have already been identified, preventive action might advantageously start from the vantage point of difficulties which need to be dealt with or situations which require correction. Such action will not be outside the framework of family values and goals, for meaningful intervention which hopes to get the family's full cooperation must be carried out within a value-goal context. Of course, obvious problematic functioning would tend to dictate an early strategy of problem solving or secondary prevention, only later giving way to primary prevention or work around the issues of family values and aspirations.

To be classified Adequate or Near Adequate in our scheme, a family must be well organized, must satisfactorily carry out its various socially expected tasks and must be able to cope with daily problems. Adequate families like to think that their own resources are sufficient for coping with their problems without help from the outside. [12] Adequate families, it may safely be assumed, are more future oriented than problem families[13] simply because their coping skills have been developed relative to situations which they anticipated and for which they prepared themselves.

Given this kind of orientation the emphasis in intervention ought to be upon the enhancement of social functioning. [14] The primary approach in working with the family would be educational rather than remedial[15] and would be inherently more positive and broader in conception than the public health concept of primary prevention which, after all, has as its referent specific diseases or pathologies. The educational approach to preventing social malfunctioning is largely neglected in the field of social work. In the broadest sense, prevention with an educational perspective begins with the assumption that all family members have aspirations. It then seeks to identify these aspirations and to relate them to the developmental tasks facing the family, the capacity of family members to carry out these tasks and to realize their goals. The educational approach attempts to explore, with the family, new ways of gaining satisfactions through the acquisition of new knowledge and skills, particularly in the fields of recreation and culture, through the enhancement of social participation in the community, through the promotion of individual and collective self-expression appropriate to individual ability and need, and through a host of other techniques.

At the same time the notion that the family is a system needing to guard itself against possible malfunctioning is played down; instead the theme of positive action in response to family growth and development and ever changing life situation and needs is emphasized. From the point of view of prevention, such action may be likened to a process of generalized immunization rather than the technique which uses a special serum for the prevention of a specific disease. Enhancement of social functioning as defined here is no more than a broad concept which requires translation into a variety of empirically developed techniques. The present social functioning analysis is only a first step in this direction.

(b) Intervention with Near Problematic families must be planned with their specific characteristics in mind, namely the fact that these families reveal problems in the intra- and interpersonal areas and in instrumental behavior as well, particularly in economic practices. By and large, the well-being of family members is not seriously impaired and stresses on family life are apt to be moderate. Family members have adaptive skills and/or access to some resources which enable them, at least temporarily, to keep the problem from seriously jeopardizing family unity and the physical or emotional health of family members.

The degree to which they are able to cope and the level at which they resolve their problems are crucial considerations for treatment planning. Service would be geared to greater depth than that proposed for the preceding group. In addition to a resolution of crises and relief from immediate distress, the social worker will attempt to educate the family regarding the pattern of behavior which gave rise to problems and to effect some modification of the problematic behavior patterns through a variety of approaches fitted to the client's situation. Techniques may include changing the role performance of family members, changing their adaptive patterns and allocating new roles wherever the social structure permits it. In some instances the social worker, through his broker role, will be able to modify role norms.

Intervention at the second level of treatment, in contrast to the previous one, calls for more intensive services: counselling for problems of behavior and interpersonal relations; more extensive effort at getting the family to make fuller and better use of community resources; innovative services when a scarcity of resources makes it impossible to meet family needs; help to change interactional patterns in the family and also with the extended family, friends, neighbors, and employers. Where the social environment is particularly unfavorable and inflexible, intervention of this sort may require the family to make changes in living arrangements or employment.

The direct association found between family malfunctioning and socio-economic status has special implications for intervention in Near Problematic families. It means, in effect, that for these families there is a special need to explore the nexus between intra-familial malfunctioning and unemployment, inadequate income, debts, financial worries, and poor housing. These may be the issues that need to be given priority, with emphasis on such tangible services as job training, job finding, provision of day care services, supplementation of public assistance payment and procurement of better housing. Health problems did not figure prominently among the young families in the sample, but there may be individual cases where there is need for health services.

Attitudes of alienation from society were found to be linked with malfunctioning in the lower class of society.

Alienation, while not a desirable state of mind, may have as its most serious feature the fact that it is diagnostic of a present or future inability to turn to resources beyond the family in time of need. Where Near Problematic families are characterized by attitudes of alienation, intervention should address itself to the development of social skills in family members--possibly by persuading them to participate in socializing activities, such as are offered at clubs, community centers, social action groups, churches. Intervention should include efforts to effect a rapprochement between client and institution, dealing with both in order to see that the social, emotional, and physical needs of the young families are met. It may be that a concerted effort to modify client attitudes will be required before feelings of alienation are modified so that the family can respond to services or other forms of community assistance. Techniques for changing attitudes will vary greatly in keeping with the family's past experience and psychological disposition. Nevertheless, they are likely to include services and activities emphasizing verbal communication, as well as concrete assistance, as a means of altering the client's negative image of the social structure.

The family functioning profile of the Near Problematic family suggests the use of an intervention strategy that puts emphasis, initially at least, upon secondary prevention. The social functioning picture reveals some problem areas that need immediate attention in order to prevent their intensification, with consequent weakening of the family's general social functioning. The Family Life Improvement Project will seek to test the hypothesis that intervention with a problem solving focus is indeed prevention. However, from our limited experience in working with young families it seems clear that even with Near Problematic clients, service must go beyond the problem solving stage. They, no less than Adequate and Near Adequate families, have values and aspirations which they seek to realize; but they lack the skill, the experience, and the assurance that make realization probable.

The combination of lower socio-economic status and greater problemicity calls, as it does in the case of more adequately functioning families, for a careful exploration of family goals. But the task of matching intervention programming with goals in this group of families is vastly more complicated for two reasons: (1) Their values and goals may be a handicap to better functioning and greater life satisfac-

tion; (2) social workers who carry out a program of intervention may, by virtue of their predominantly middle-class
background, have a bias against values and goals considered
lower class.

Although professional social work has made some
progress in identifying and counteracting the built-in status
bias inherent in practice, it is doubtful that bias, which is
the product of social status differences, can ever be elimi-
nated. The helping professions should promote understanding of the life styles of the sub-cultures to be served and
should cultivate acceptance and respect for differences.

An attitude of rigorous non-judgmentalism may, however, stand in the way of recognizing that "a number of
these patterns (of the poor or disorganized) tend to operate
to the disadvantage of them."[16] On this the intervenor is
not likely to be guided by any hard and fast rules. Patterns
of behavior that deviate from community norms must be seen
vis-a-vis their consequences. If the family has a casual approach toward unplanned pregnancies but is ill equipped to
support and socialize more children, family planning may
have to be made a focal point of intervention.

Yet, any attempt at correcting idiosyncratically deviant or sub-culturally determined patterns of behavior must
be carried out within the context of affirmative socialization. This includes helping the family to identify goals and
to consider alternative means for attaining them, thus finding
ways to enhance the satisfaction of family members by way
of social participation, recreation, the practice of skills,
etc.

(c) Intervention to improve the social functioning of
Problematic families starts from the empirically based
premise that this more extreme form of malfunctioning constitutes an interlocking of malfunctioning in many areas--
Family Relationships, Individual Behavior, Care and Treatment of Children, Social Activities, and instrumental areas,
particularly Economic and Household Practices. Some of
these families are truly multi-problem in that their functioning represents a threat to the well-being of one or more
family members. Others show behavior that is potentially
dangerous to family welfare.

As family relations are of a problematic nature in
87% of cases, the high proportion (56%) of malfunctioning

in Individual Behavior and Adjustment may be seen as an
underlying factor in the defective pattern of relationships.
Intervention to cope with these more serious intra-personal
and interpersonal problems requires intensive counseling
and, in cases of serious pathology, referral for specialized
treatment.

Problematic families, with few exceptions, are deprived families. Poor household practices (in 50% of the
cases), which reflect generally sub-standard housing conditions, are a special area of concern. So are problems in
the economic area. Here, as in the Near Problematic
group, the most appropriate strategy of service may be
early assistance to improve the housing and economic situation. Help with these matters can open the door for intervention in areas of Individual Behavior and Family Relationships, as well as Care and Training of Children.

Because of the rather problematic nature of baby
care in these families, it would seem desirable for workers
to invest time and effort in attempts to help the mothers
improve their child care and training practices. The high
scores on the PARI scales made by mothers of malfunctioning families from the lower classes suggests that there is
need for informal child care instruction and demonstration
at home or at neighborhood clinics. Young Mothers' Clubs
are another alternative for dealing with the problem of
child care in the Problematic group of families.

Widespread socio-economic deprivation in the Problematic group calls for a program of intervention backed by
resources to increase economic security and to raise the
standard of living. Where earning potential is absent or
limited, an income maintenance program must be made
available. Beyond that, deprived and malfunctioning families need to experience a degree of achievement and success
in family life. The social worker can help them achieve
this goal by giving active guidance, perhaps even performing certain tasks that are beyond the competence of the family, at least until they are learned and incorporated through
imitation. The importance of a role model provided from
the outside cannot be overemphasized in view of the significant correlation between the malfunctioning of the young
families and their respective families of orientation. As in
the Near Problematic families, intervention here will maxi-
mize efforts to help the families establish a connection with
the larger social structure of the community so as to reduce

isolation and bring about better use of resources.

Intervention with the Problematic as well as the Near
Problematic group of families often means providing the
economic, social, and emotional props for the single or deserted mother, whether she lives alone or with parents or
relatives.   Her functioning was found to be significantly
more problematic than that of the married mother in the
same status group.   Service to the unmarried or deserted
mother will utilize some or all of the techniques used in
working with those who have husbands, but casework is
likely to focus especially upon problems inherent in the
single mother's relationship to the social network.   For
mothers living in social isolation the establishment of activity and educational peer groups may be indicated.

All in all, intervention in the lives of Problematic
families, contrasting with treatment for Adequate and Near
Adequate families, calls for a heavy reliance upon service
in the instrumental areas.   While the cause and effect relationship between malfunctioning in expressive behavior--the
term is used here to denote areas of intra- and extra-
familial relationships--and instrumental behavior remains
hypothetical, our program of intervention is guided by an
assumption of the greater vulnerability to overall problem
functioning of the instrumentally handicapped families. [17]
However, the approach which advocates beginning treatment
by helping the client with tangible problems that he himself
has clearly identified has long been preferred by social
workers serving the economically deprived population.

The initial emphasis of preventive intervention to
Problematic families must be on secondary or even tertiary
(rehabilitative) prevention.   Evidence of substantial malfunctioning in four or more areas of family functioning under-
scores the need for dealing first with the prime obstacles
to normal existence and development.   Diagnostic and treatment intervention aimed at removing such obstacles should
lead to a discovery of the sub-strata of family functioning
which, as in the case of less malfunctioning families, comprises a core of values, hopes, and aspirations.

Work with truly Problematic families may never be
able to shift its focus to primary prevention but may need
to remain a mainly remedial or rehabilitative service.
This would be especially true for chronically malfunctioning
cases whose response to professional intervention might be

limited to only minor modifications in the functioning pattern. By contrast, in work with Problematic families which show what Reuben Hill has called "the roller-coaster profile of adjustment (crisis-disorganization-recovery-reorganization),"[18] there is a fair chance that treatment might take on the character of primary prevention as families are helped to emerge from the low point of the crisis profile. The helping professions are in dire need of information on longitudinal patterns of family functioning as a basis for a focused planning of preventive services.

The inter-generational comparison of the social functioning of suburban families (see Table 15) represents a first effort to view prevention from an empirical change perspective. The comparison, in spite of its obvious shortcomings when compared to longitudinal research, gave support to the study's working hypothesis which postulates that some change toward less adequate functioning is an inherent part of family development. Socio-economic status clearly emerged as one of the variables influencing the nature of this change. The cross-sectional analysis of samples of young families suggests that many other social and psychological factors related to the static level of social functioning have a hand in shaping the nature of family development.

The typology sketched above and supported by an analysis of empirical and reasonably representative data remains a highly generalized formulation of intervention techniques to be employed with young families which differ in their degree of social malfunctioning. Because of the present state of knowledge, a more precise formulation, which correlates the quantitative picture (typology) of family malfunctioning with specific service strategies, cannot be predetermined. It is one of the hoped for outcomes of a long-range program of research aimed at preventive intervention.

Notes

1. Geismar and LaSorte, op. cit. , p. 88, ff.

2. Ibid. , p. 58-59.

3. Geismar, "Family Functioning as an Index of Need for Welfare Services," loc. cit. , p. 104-109. The family functioning profiles of these two family groups are shown on page 104 of this article.

4. The younger families were selected at random from
    the register of first births to mothers under 30 which
    occurred within one year.   The older families repre-
    sent a random selection of families who have at least
    one child in the sixth grade of a school serving the
    total community.

5. Knowledge about the socio-economic mobility of
    families leaves no room for the assumption that fami-
    lies in this community tend to be downward mobile.
    The relative distribution of racial and religious char-
    acteristics in the two age groups suggests we are
    dealing with different populations.   The reasons for
    the differences can only be guessed.   They may be
    sought in a selective out-migration of upward mobile
    families.   Although the city of New Brunswick is
    suburban in character, it has the reputation of offer-
    ing more limited opportunities in housing and public
    education to middle-class families than do most of
    the surrounding communities.   Objective indices of
    such a difference are hard to come by, but census
    data on median income and condition of housing sup-
    port the above supposition.   See U. S. Censuses of
    Population and Housing: 1960 Final Report PHC (1)-
    91 Middlesex County, N. J.   Bureau of the Census,
    U. S. Department of Commerce.

6. Irwin D. J. Bross, Design for Decision.   New York,
    The MacMillan Company, 1953, p. 34-35.

7. Ibid., p. 34.

8. Geismar, LaSorte, and Ayres, op. cit.

9. Thanks are due to Jane Krisberg for help in writing
    this section.

10. Charles F. Grosser, "Community Development Pro-
    grams Serving the Urban Poor," Social Work, Vol.
    X, No. 3, July, 1965, p. 15-21.

11. Howard Parad, loc. cit., p. 287.

12. I am indebted to Professor Herbert Aptekar of
    Brandeis University for the ideas expressed here.

13.   Ibid.

14.   Ibid.

15.   Ibid.

16.   Catherine S. Chilman, Growing Up Poor. Washington, D. C., U. S. Department of Health, Education and Welfare, Welfare Administration, 1966.

17.   Geismar, "Family Functioning as an Index for Need for Welfare Services," loc. cit.

18.   Reuben Hill, "Generic Features of Families Under Stress," Crisis Intervention, ed. Howard J. Parad, op. cit., p. 32-52, p. 46.

Chapter 4
Preventive Intervention at Three Levels of
Family Functioning--Three Case Studies

In order to verify the foregoing formulations on
strategies of early intervention, summaries of three cases
that have been receiving preventive services from the Rutgers University Family Life Improvement Project are presented below.   These cases are part of a sample of 230
randomly selected young urban families, which constitute the
treatment group in the project.   There are two reasons why
we chose these particular families for illustrative purposes:
1. each one represents a different level of family functioning corresponding to the three broad levels identified in the
previous chapter as focal points for planning preventive intervention;   2. their histories show patterns of intervention
which differ from each other in the emphasis on discussion
content and the use of community resources.

Since a comprehensive analysis of all the treatment
data is lacking, no claim is made that these cases are representative of the total treatment population.   At this point
in the action phase of the project there is no way of determining representativeness.   On the other hand, the criterion
for choosing these three families was not success; to the
contrary, quite a number of project clients have shown
more movement during the treatment period than the selected three.   In choosing them, however, we did seek to
avoid those few situations in which the social worker had
failed to establish a relationship with the client.

The question of success and failure in social work
preventive intervention can only be treated meaningfully
from a long-term perspective, with treatment outcome
viewed relative to treatment goals.   The previous sections
of this monograph and the present case studies do address
themselves to the formulation of appropriate treatment goals,
while descriptions of actual intervention are designed to illustrate the application of such goals to specific family situations.   The question of outcome can only be dealt with af-

ter services have been completed and within the context of
a research design which permits a statistical comparison of
treatment with non-treatment cases.

These three illustrative cases are discussed by juxta-
posing family situation and pattern of intervention. The former revolves around the dimension family functioning and,
as noted, the cases represent three distinct dimensional
levels. Pattern of intervention is concerned with areas of
focus, the frequency and nature of client-worker interaction,
the process of family socialization into the client role and
other treatment variables.

The professional intervention given the three families
takes the form of a service they had not received earlier
and which is not readily available to others. To avoid mis-
understanding, we ought to add that this type of intervention
is not available to the public as a preventive service, although it is, on occasion, given to families which have been
a community concern or have sought--and actually found--
treatment because of strong motivation.

Although the question of treatment utility cannot be
answered (at least in relation to objective outcome criteria)
the case studies supply concrete evidence that the social
functioning patterns of young families allow room for social
work services, and that such families tend to respond positively to these services when they become available. The
profile narrative on the families, which appears in summary
form, is not to be viewed as a comprehensive family study
or a diagnosis in depth, but rather as a systematic analysis
of some basic psycho-social dimensions of family life seen
as relevant to preventive planning.

The three families may be viewed as characterizing
the family functioning levels of our earlier broad categori-
zation--Near Adequate, Near Problematic, and Problematic
--and they will be presented in this order. Although they
represent actual treatment cases, all identifying information has been disguised to preserve the individual's anonym-
ity. The data on the families are being presented within
the framework of the Profile of Family Functioning used in
this study.

The "G." Family as an Illustration of
Near Adequate Social Functioning
Social Functioning Preceding Intervention[1]

A. Family Relationships and Family Unity

This is a family of three consisting of husband, wife,
and infant child. Mr. and Mrs. G. were married in March,
1963, when he was 28 and she was 19, one year after meeting on a blind date arranged by mutual friends. Both families had approved of their plans and their courtship period
was happy, each partner enjoying the personal qualities of
the other. Since their marriage, however, there has been
difficulty over their relationship with Mr. G.'s mother, in
whose home the young couple lived during the early months
of their marriage. At that time Mrs. G. became resentful
of the demands made upon her by her mother-in-law and also of her husband's attitude toward his mother. Even though
she described how upset he was over the difficulty, she felt
he was unable to oppose his mother in any way. Mrs. G.
became nervous over the situation, there was open conflict
between the two women, and as a result the young couple
moved to their own apartment, where the in-law problem
became more attenuated.

They were thrilled when their son, Roger, was born
in 1964. Mrs. G. considered her husband good both as a
breadwinner and father and gave the impression that he re-
spected her efficiency as a wife, housekeeper, and mother.
She was pleased with her marriage in spite of the problems
with her mother-in-law. Her marriage expectations were
"having a baby and an apartment," and these she had. On
his part, Mr. G. was satisfied that his wife did not object
to his "going out with the boys."

Prior to the birth of their son their sexual relationship had been mutually satisfactory. However, Mrs. G. indicated that since then she has not been really interested in
sex, and that her husband feels she should have relations
with him more often. She mentioned that he becomes an-
gry at her refusal but only for a short period of time. As
for contraception, they have not used it in any form.

Mr. and Mrs. G. seem genuinely fond of each other
and enjoy being together, including their baby in the weekly
outing which is one of their main forms of recreation.
Both partners derive great satisfaction from their parental
roles. Mr. G. has broken his formerly close relationship

with his mother and now visits her only in the company of his wife and baby.

Mrs. G. is a rather nervous person who tends to manipulate her husband by crying and complaining of illness. While the two enjoy talking together, they communicate little or not at all on such matters as sex and their feelings about their lives in general. Despite this, they seem to be very much attached to each other and to their son; their relationship with him is a major source of family strength.

B. Individual Behavior and Adjustment

Mr. G. was born in 1935 in Newark of immigrant parents. His father was of Italian-Catholic origin and his mother was Protestant. His father died of cancer at the age of 33, and Mr. G. has no memory of him. The youngest of three children, Mr. G. was close to his brother, a solidarity born of their mother's preference for their sister. But after the two older children married and left home, the mother began to depend heavily upon him. He worked part-time while in high school to help at home, and his mother encouraged a close, dependent relationship. On the other hand, he was not isolated; he had many friends in school, was active in sports, and enjoyed being in military service from 1958-60, when he was stationed in Korea.

Mr. G. seems to function well as a father, husband, and breadwinner. He has many friends and, although somewhat shy, gets along well with people. He has been able to mitigate his dependent relationship with his mother to his wife's satisfaction, but he probably still has conflict in this area.

Mrs. G. was born in 1943 in Newark of a Catholic, lower middle-class, American-born family, and has always had a pleasant relationship with her parents. She has one brother with whom she has become close since both have married. At the age of fifteen she started dating and has always had a large clique of friends. In her senior year she dropped out of high school to become employed full-time, an action she later regretted.

The interviewer described Mrs. G. as being a slim, well-groomed, relaxed person of average intelligence with a friendly and hospitable manner who enjoys having people around. This impression was somewhat contrary to her own self-description, for she pictures herself as being nervous, a description largely confirmed by further observation and the collection of diagnostic data (see G). The interviewer thought that she has difficulty in expressing anger and acknowledging unpleasant feelings.

C. Care and Training of Children

Roger is a well built baby of normal development who is following a regular schedule and shows signs of good care. Mrs. G. expects to assume most of the responsibility for disciplining him as he gets older and plans to raise him in much the same way she herself was raised, stressing respect for adults, good manners, etc. Her husband has agreed that she can carry this responsibility. She appears relaxed when discussing plans for the child's future care, such as feeding, toilet training, etc. She plans to start toilet training at the age of nine months, but she states that she would be patient if it took time. She believes in discipline and feels that, when necessary, spanking gets the best results.

Mrs. G. was observed to speak warmly to the baby and to show pleasure when he responded to her. However, the interviewer also noticed that she does not handle him much; she will prop the bottle and declare somewhat defensively that he either sleeps or stays in his playpen much of the time and was "not one for arms."

D. Social Activities

The G.'s visit each of their families weekly and always take the baby with them. They socialize with two couples, eating at each other's homes and going to drive-in movies with their children. With Mr. G.'s brother and family they go on outings, such as picnics and day trips to the shore. Mr. G. bowls once a week with a group of co-workers and attends meetings of the food store employees' union; although he is not an active member he enjoys it because it affords him an opportunity to be with friends. Mrs. G. expresses no interest in organized groups but visits informally with friends and neighbors.

E. Economic Practices

Mr. G. is employed as a dairy clerk at a large supermarket, a company for which he has worked in varying capacities since he was fifteen years old. He likes his work, for which his net pay is $97.00 a week, and finds his job status satisfactory.

Mrs. G. is the family's money manager, an arrangement entirely to Mr. G.'s liking, for she is a very careful purchaser and prudent planner. They rarely spend money on entertainment and seem to manage well without a strict budget, although monthly provisions are made for the purchase of food, payment of rent, insurance, and other necessities. There are no debts, and savings acquired with the aid of small monthly deposits in a credit union amount to $1,500.00.

F. Household Practices

The G.'s live in a three-room apartment in a multifamily building. There is a crowded appearance to the apartment for the washing machine is kept in the center hall, the living room also serves as a dining room, the playpen takes up a large part of this living area and the baby shares the parents' room. They feel the apartment is too small and hope to move, perhaps to a house in the suburbs, although they are unsure of their ability to finance such an undertaking.

Mrs. G. manages all the household chores by herself, performing the routine work daily so the apartment stays neat. Though unpretentious, it is kept very clean and displays warmth through pictures and mementoes.

G. Health Conditions and Practices

Mr. G. and Roger are both in excellent physical health. Mr. G. visits the family doctor when necessary and Roger has monthly checkups. Both Mr. and Mrs. G. get regular dental care.

Mrs. G. has a number of complaints, several of which appear to be psychosomatic in origin. She takes pills because she has had what she describes as a heart

murmur since the birth of the baby.   She has had bad back
pains from time to time as a result of falling on the ice.
She also has some internal problems, which she ascribes
to a difficult delivery.   The physician who examines Roger
checks her monthly.   She describes herself as having periodic "nervous breakdowns" which consist of dizziness, loss
of appetite, nervousness, and temper tantrums, owing to
her "in-law problem."   Mrs. G. repeatedly states that she
has to "take it easy" because of her health.

H. Use of Community Resources

Mrs. G. seems to place high value on education.
She wishes to select Roger's school, preferably a parochial
school, carefully.   Before the baby was born Mrs. G. attended the Catholic church each week; now the parents attend together once a month although Mr. G. is not a Catholic.   Prior to their marriage the G.'s attended some meetings on sex and married life at the church.   At the time of
the first interview Mrs. G. was not aware of the health and
social resources in the city and was pleased to be told about
them.   She indicated that she might possibly use a family
agency to help her with her problems concerning Mr. G.'s
mother.

The G.'s are a lower middle-class family which, on
the quantitative scale of values used in this study, may be
characterized as belonging to the upper, Near Adequate, end
of the continuum.   They have a limited income but it appears to satisfy present needs.   Their achievements are not
out of line with their aspirations, and there is no evidence
of status frustration.   Mrs. G. is the dominant partner who
is able to determine the nature of relationships with respect
to child-rearing, sex, and contact with the mother-in-law.
She uses illness and crying spells as a means of controlling
her husband.   Yet, this situation does not seriously upset
the substantial degree of social equilibrium found in the G.
family.

The G.'s face some problems--as do most families--
but at this point the problems pose no serious threat to family well-being and unity.   Although the wife appears to have
her way on matters which are important to her, including
relationships with the in-laws, she is preoccupied with the
mother-in-law situation and not completely sure of her husband's ultimate loyalty.   Mrs. G.'s somewhat delicate state

of health requires continuous attention and financial outlays.
Her minor illnesses, probably of psychosomatic origin, enable her to wield a disproportionate influence in several
areas of decision making.

Pattern of Intervention

The Family Life Improvement Project, as stated
earlier, did not operate according to any predetermined and
articulated pattern of intervention in family situations.   Instead, the project had some broad treatment guidelines
(see previous section) suggesting frequency of contact and
the areas of social functioning most likely to need professional attention.   These guidelines were helpful in developing a treatment plan for each individual family which, save
for some inevitable modifications arising in a treatment situation, was followed in the rendering of services.   The present write-up, illustrating types of intervention rather than
treatment itself, will not differentiate between treatment
plan and service but be confined to a summary description
of the actual service given.

The G.'s family situation does not call for any major and urgent problem solving by the social worker. Their
instrumental needs are reasonably well met, and the family
faces no serious crises in interpersonal relationships or
the social-emotional behavior of family members.   Nonetheless, Mrs. G.'s psychosomatic problems were seen as de-
serving professional attention.   The prevention-oriented
worker was planning to see this family bi-monthly unless
the need arose for more frequent contact.   The emphasis
was likely to be on helping Mrs. G. to attain a better state
of emotional health, on an enhancement of the total family's
social functioning, and on exploring ways of realizing family goals and gaining greater satisfaction in family living.

The process of involving the G.'s in a treatment
service was surprisingly uncomplicated.   Preceded by a research interview designed to establish the level of family
functioning and a letter informing the family that they were
selected for the treatment group in this University-run research project, the first visit by the social worker was met
with interest and friendliness on the part of the wife.
Throughout the period of treatment the family remained cooperative and eager to continue the relationship with the social worker.

An analysis of Treatment Log[2] data showed that the
worker had ten in-person contacts with the G. family over
a 15 month period.   In other words, the family was seen
somewhat more often than had been scheduled, because a
number of problems arose in the course of rendering service. On two occasions these called for successive contacts
on a weekly basis.   During these periods of greater activity
two of the contacts were initiated by the client, but the
worker took the initiative in eight contacts.   The issues
which gave rise to greater activity were a husband-wife relationship crisis centering around Mr. G.'s presumed dependency on his mother and an effort by the G.'s, in which
they enlisted the help of the worker, to improve their housing situation.   Mrs. G. was seen most often, but the husband was seen separately on two occasions and once jointly
with his wife.

Exploration by worker and discussion between worker
and client were the main modes of intervention.   Practical
help from the worker and worker contact with community
resources on behalf of the client were not utilized because
the family appeared to be quite able to help itself in instrumental matters and to reach out to the resources which
were needed.   Discussion was most frequently focused on
family relationships, particularly the husband-wife relationship, with family health and the housing situation ranking
second and third in frequency.   A variety of other subjects,
such as child care, social activities, and financial management, also entered into the client-worker conversations, but
with a lower frequency.   Greater frequency of discussion in
the G. case is broadly correlated with degree of problemicity of a given subject.

Service to the family was at least partly characterized by an educational emphasis.   The social worker engaged the family in discussion on child development, training of children, child spacing, and household management,
all areas which, in this family, constituted issues of interest rather than areas of concern.   But by and large, client-
worker discussions in this Near Adequate family were domi-
nated by a sufficient number of minor crises to make intervention more problem-centered than educational.

Changes During Treatment

During the fifteen months of service (not completed
at the time of reporting) a number of changes occurred in
the family's social functioning. These are summarized below. The present report identifies those areas of functioning in which the worker concentrated intervention, but no attempt is made to assess the relative effect of this intervention. Mrs. G. became pregnant by design and a second
child, Bonnie, was born after a difficult pregnancy. Both
children are developing normally although Roger suffers from
bronchial attacks for which he had to be hospitalized on one
occasion. Despite medical advice, which discouraged the
second pregnancy, the parents are planning to have four children. Their sex life is described as satisfactory. Mrs. G.
complains frequently about her husband's indecisiveness and
continues to direct him in all matters of importance to her.
There is more verbal communication between husband and
wife, and they tend to talk things over when they are an-
noyed. The worker has been concentrating her efforts in
this area. Communication has also increased between Mrs.
G. and her mother-in-law, encouraged by the social worker
who sought to guide the G.'s away from conspiracy and toward direct contact. While this has enabled Mrs. G. to
feel less tense, the mother-in-law problem continues to occupy her periodically.

Mrs. G., bored by the confinement in the home, had
at one point taken a job as a cosmetics saleswoman but gave
it up because she found the work too taxing. Mr. G.'s
salary has been rising gradually, but not much more than
the rise in cost-of-living. The presence of a second child
and the need to contribute some financial support to a sick
relative causes the family to feel the financial pinch more
than at the onset of treatment. This situation recently led
Mr. G. to cancel, without prior consultation with his wife,
a contract for the purchase of a suburban home. No money
was lost in the transaction. Mrs. G. views Mr. G.'s action with much ambivalence. She is terribly upset about not
being consulted and suspects that her mother-in-law had a
hand in this. On the other hand, she is pleased by this
seeming evidence of his ability to make a quick and important decision. At the end of the treatment period covered
by the Log, the G.'s have found an interim solution to their
housing problem. They have moved in with Mrs. G.'s parents, who own a large home in which the young family will

occupy more spacious quarters than they have in their present apartment.   The children will have more room for in-
door and outdoor play than they have at present.   This plan
avoids the financial strain which would have attended the
purchase of a home at this point.

The "B." Family, an Illustration of
Near Problematic Social Functioning

Social Functioning Preceding Intervention

A. Family Relationships and Family Unity

Mr. and Mrs. B. have been married since April,
1963.   Although never formally engaged, they went steady
for a year before they married.   Their families were known
to each other before the marriage and were satisfied with
their choice.   Both husband and wife were employed at the
time of marriage, but Mr. B. suffered a heart attack several months later which forced him to stop working.   Mrs.
B. continued to work for almost a year but left the job when
she became pregnant.   Their first child was born in February, 1965, and Mrs. B. was again pregnant at the time of
the initial interview.   The B.'s planned to have four children and did not consider using any form of birth control.
Mrs. B. indicated that she and her husband both enjoyed
their sexual relationship.

As the oldest child in her parents' home, Mrs. B.
had assumed responsibility for the care of her siblings and
the household and, therefore, thought that she knew what was
expected of her as a wife.   She was rather vague about how
much knowledge she had of sex before marriage, but indicated that the sources of information were her mother and
her friends.

Mr. and Mrs. B. were both pleased with the first
pregnancy; they wanted children immediately and hold the
view that the purpose of marriage is to raise a family.
Although Mr. B. had expressed a preference for a boy, he
was pleased when a daughter was born.

The B.'s seem fairly content but somewhat apathetic
in their relationship with each other.   They are very much
involved with the husband's extended family and spend a
great deal of time with them, an arrangement which is sat-

isfying to both of them.   Mrs. B. generally shows a lack
of affection but is accepting of all aspects of their life, including her husband's physical condition and his inability to
work.   She stated in the interview that they had no areas of
disagreement and that the few decisions they have to make
are made jointly.   More extended contact with the family,
however, revealed that Mrs. B. is satisfied to let her husband make most of the decisions.   The partners to this marriage neither receive, nor do they expect much verbal communication or emotional support from one another.   Mr. B.
wants his wife to keep the house neat, sleep with him, and
bear his children, while Mrs. B.'s expectation is only that
he be the father of her children.

     The main ties between the couple are their daughter,
Mr. B.'s family, and their shared love of rock and roll mu-
sic.   They go to the movies about once a month but sometimes leave in the middle of the picture because the husband
becomes tired.   The B.'s take their meals, shop, and watch
television together, while other activities tend to be shared
with the extended family.   The baby also spends much time
with Mr. B.'s parents and receives much affection from
them.   This strong attachment and involvement with the extended B. family makes it appear that they all form a joint
family unit.   The young folks seem content with this arrangement, and there is no evidence of conflict between them on
this issue.

B. Individual Behavior and Adjustment

     Mrs. B., who was born in 1942, is of Italian, Ro-
man Catholic background.   She is of medium height and build,
slightly cross-eyed, looking older than her age.   At the
time of the first interview her physical appearance was un-
tidy, for she had just set her freshly dyed hair.   A speech
defect makes it somewhat difficult to understand her speech.
Her manner is apathetic, and in social situations, she gives
the impression of being helpless and lost.   She was non-
verbal, nervous and fidgety during the interview and seemed
unable to think in terms of the family's future.   Although a
graduate of high school she reads with difficulty, and one is
left to conclude that her intelligence is below normal.   However, she exhibits genuine strengths in her role as housekeeper and mother, as evidenced by the very well-kept
apartment and the excellent physical care bestowed on her
daughter.

Mr. B. was born in 1940, also of Italian, Roman Catholic descent. He is about 5' 7' with a heavy build and a quiet manner, also looking much older than his age. His tested intelligence is subnormal (I.Q. 72), but he has high manual dexterity and has shown interest in cooking and beauty culture. Mr. B. had two heart attacks, September and December, 1964, for which he was hospitalized. At the present time he is under regular clinic care. An 8th grade graduate, Mr. B. was a machine operator before he became ill; now is dependent for resources on the community, his parents, and relatives.

He expresses dissatisfaction over being on welfare and would prefer gainful employment.

Neither Mr. or Mrs. B. are interested in organized activities or community affairs. Neither are known to have been involved in anti-social behavior.

C. Care and Training of Children

Debbie appears to be a normal, happy, healthy, baby of seven months, enjoying the attention she receives from all members of her large, extended family. At the time of the initial interview she had cut two teeth and her mother complained that she was cranky. Her physical development is advanced; she can crawl and pull herself up to a standing position. She shows evidence of good physical care, is bathed daily, is suitably clothed and adequately fed. As an infant she was bottle-fed on a demand schedule; now she eats baby foods. Her physical health had been safeguarded by regular clinic visits.

Mrs. B. believes that Debbie is spoiled because there is always someone to pick her up when she cries. Mr. and Mrs. B. have never discussed discipline, but Mrs. B. thinks both parents should discipline a child and that children should be spanked when naughty. The father, however, does not discipline Debbie, while the mother's method of disciplining is handslapping, especially if the child pulls hair or reaches for things she shouldn't have, yet the mother is not consistent in this. Mrs. B. is eager for Debbie to walk and to be toilet trained, for she dislikes changing diapers and she is confident that the baby will learn quickly because she is so active. The worker noticed, however, that Mrs. B. had no clear idea on how to go about weaning and toilet training the child.

D. Social Activities

As noted above, the B.'s live in close proximity to
Mr. B.'s family and enjoy a warm, congenial relationship.
They are also friendly with the neighbors in the house.
There is no such close relationship with Mrs. B.'s family;
a good deal of bad feeling has existed between them since
the wife's parents tried to break up the marriage in the
wake of Mr. B.'s heart attacks, and social contacts occur
once a month at the most.   The B.'s have no desire to join
outside groups or organizations.

E. Economic Practices

The B.'s receive a city public welfare grant amount-
ing to $168.50 per month.   They do not complain about this
amount and feel they have what they need and want.   There
are no savings, no bank account, no insurance or other as-
sets, but also no debts.   Their appliances were bought before their marriage, and they have made few purchases
since then.   Occasional material aid from Mr. B.'s family
makes it easier for them to manage on their limited budget.

When Mr. B. was employed he netted $60-70 weekly.
As mentioned before, Mrs. B. was employed before her
first pregnancy.

F. Home and Household Practices

The B. family lives in an old apartment house in a
deteriorated neighborhood.   The house, with dirty, dingy
halls, is in poor condition and infested with mice and
roaches.   The B.'s occupy four adequately furnished rooms,
with the parents and child sharing a common bedroom.   The
apartment is cheerfully and imaginatively decorated, an
achievement of which Mrs. B. is proud.   It is also neat and
well-kept, with new appliances and adequate privacy.   Since
Mr. B. is on a salt-free diet, Mrs. B. prepares food for
them both, eating whatever her husband does, invariably
taking her meals with him.

G. Health Conditions and Practices

Mr. B. has a chronic heart condition and the medical prognosis is poor. He is not able to work, needs to have frequent rest, and is allowed to climb stairs only once a day. He is on a special salt-free diet and expected to go to the clinic for medical care once every two weeks. Mr. B., who dislikes the clinic, often fails to appear and also frequently neglects to follow the doctor's advice on medicine and diet. This appears to be the most serious area of concern in the functioning of the family. Mrs. B. has no health problems.

Mrs. B. told the interviewer that she and the baby always follow the doctor's instructions. Debbie receives regular clinic checkups and is free of health problems. The family uses dental care only when someone is in pain.

H. Use of Community Resources

The only community resources used by the B. family are the welfare department and the clinics. Church attendance is sporadic, confined to holidays, and the couple does not necessarily attend together.

Mr. B. and the baby, as noted above, are seen at the clinics. Like her husband, Mrs. B. is unfavorably disposed toward clinics, although she seems to value the baby clinic because Debbie has enjoyed good health. Recreation agencies are not used by the family, and they express no need for such resources.

The B.'s, a lower class family, were termed Near Problematic because they face serious problems in the instrumental areas of family functioning; family relationships, however, are stable and family members exhibit a sense of unity. The father's health condition, which is most precarious, is aggravated by the fact that he is erratic about following medical advice. The family's tight budget does not allow them to change from the public clinic to which he is assigned to a medical setting which he might like better. Neither parent has any idea about ways of improving their economic situation; they are unaware of community resources which might aid in areas of income, health, and housing. The family derives much strength from their close relationship with the extended family. Mr. B. is the dominant part-

ner in a stable marital relationship, and with the consistent
support of his wife, he has stood up well under the stress
of serious illness and transition from gainful employment to
enforced idleness.

Pattern of Intervention

While this analysis was being done the B. family had
been in treatment for 16 months; the service had involved
28 home visits, three visits to agencies, and 66 phone contacts with the family and collaterals. Husband and wife
were seen together 17 times, the wife separately 20 times,
and the husband alone 11 times. [3] Moreover, relatives of
the family were seen on two occasions. During the second
half of the service period when treatment was concerned
with a full assessment of Mr. B.'s disability and rehabilitation services for him, the husband was seen alone with
the same frequency as the wife. During the first eight
treatment months, contacts were initiated by the worker,
rather than the client, at the ratio of 18 to 1. During the
second eight months, the ratio was reduced to 5 to 1, with
the husband as well as the wife initiating contact with the
worker. Unlike the G. family, whose members were more
verbal and instrumentally self-sufficient, the modes of intervention here were marked not only by exploration and discussion but by a considerable amount of advice and guidance, frequent contact with community resources, occasional non-verbal interaction, and some practical help in the
form of chauffeuring family members to the clinic.

Also in contrast to the less problematic G. case,
discussion with the B.'s was largely concentrated in the
area of Individual Behavior and Adjustment of the father,
and in the instrumental areas of economic functioning, housing, health, child care, and use of social agencies. Family
Relationships and Unity, the least frequently discussed subject, was dealt with but once, while Social Activities, particularly relationships with the extended family, and the
problem of limited social outlets for the family, came up
in discussion only four times. The service rendered by the
caseworker was heavily problem-oriented as would have been
expected in view of the fact that urgent health and economic
problems overshadowed the total family situation. The B.
family offered only mild resistance to being involved in the
project when first approached by the social worker and became very responsive to the offer of service when they

realized its potential usefulness.

    The social worker concentrated her efforts on mobil-
izing community resources to ease the B.'s economic and
housing situation and to secure proper health care for Mr.
B.   Getting the family to use community resources required a two-pronged approach: (1) Informing the family of
available resources and their eligibility requirements, moti-
vating them to use the resources, and steering them through
the jungle of red tape and bureaucracy;   (2) acting as the
family's advocate in securing services.   The latter was accomplished by interpreting family needs and problems to the
agencies and by using a variety of techniques, dependent upon the worker's prestige and knowledge of the community's
health and welfare system, to expedite action for the client's
benefit.   Endeavoring to cope with the family's problems,
the worker brought the family into contact with categorical
public assistance rather than city welfare.   These included
health and rehabilitation agencies, vocational guidance, and
Planned Parenthood.   Several other types of agencies were
used as the need arose for a particular kind of short-term
service.

    Professional intervention in the case of the B. family
can be viewed as being preventive as well as problem-solving in nature, for service directed at strengthening the instrumental areas of social functioning was designed to bolster
the social and emotional health of individuals and to prevent
a weakening of family relationships and unity.   Although at
first the B.'s were relatively apathetic toward treatment
and social and health resources, their relative psycho-social
adequacy allowed them to cooperate with the worker in dealing with those problems which exerted the greatest stress
in family living.

Change During Treatment

    A second child, Ellen, was born prematurely to the
B. family in the seventh month of pregnancy.   She weighed
only 3 lbs. 2 oz., and remained in the hospital for two
months until she reached the weight of five pounds.   After
this birth Mrs. B. used Planned Parenthood for a time but
she is again pregnant by design, for the parents are still
determined to have four children.

    Mr. B. has been taking vocational tests.   His lack

of high school education, low I. Q. , and poor health are
barriers to acceptance into a training program.   Continuing
to express dissatisfaction with the clinic, he uses a private
doctor from time to time to get medication.   He takes on
all the worries and concerns of his extended family as well
as his own.   For instance, when his younger brother was
killed in an automobile accident, Mr. B. took charge of the
funeral arrangements.

Mrs. B. , although still overshadowed by Mr. B. , has
begun to emerge as an independent personality.   She will in-
dependently discuss problems with the worker instead of
calling in her husband to supply the answers as she once did.
From the visiting nurse she has gained knowledge about nu-
trition, and she is trying to apply it to the feeding of her
children.   Debbie, the older child, has learned to get her
own way by playing parents and grandparents against one another.   Discipline continues to be inconsistent, and one
gains the impression that the child, rather than the mother,
is in control of the situation.

The B. family has been transferred from city relief
to categorical assistance, a change involving a 45% rise in
the amount of the grant.   The B. 's occupy a larger apartment in the same neighborhood, new quarters which are
more attractive and are free of roaches and mice.   One of
the most striking changes in the family's functioning has
been their use of community resources.

The "P." Family as an Illustration
of Problematic Social Functioning

Social Functioning Preceding Intervention

A. Family Relationships and Family Unity

This family consists of an unmarried teenage mother
and her daughter, born February 18, 1965.   Audrey P. , the
mother, aged 18, and her boyfriend, Lucius, who is the
father of the child, have continued to live with their respective families, and their daughter is being cared for by the
paternal relatives.

Audrey met Lucius K. at a basketball game and saw
him daily thereafter.   She stated in the first interview that
they were only intimate a few times before she became

pregnant, that her mother "felt terrible" about her pregnancy,
but that apparently Lucius' mother was more accepting of
the situation.   Audrey said that it was very common in her
crowd to have sexual relations and that it was an activity
in which all her friends engaged, although she had derived
no enjoyment from it at first.   Although her mother had in-
formed her about birth control she had not used it.   Her
older sister had also borne an out-of-wedlock child.

Prior to her pregnancy Audrey had attended the local
public high school, dropping out after completing the 11th
grade.   At the time of the interview she was enrolled in a
Youth Corps Training Program.   Her boyfriend had also
dropped out of school after finishing the ninth grade.   They
have no resources and are, therefore, dependent upon their
parents.   Although they see each other almost daily and
continue to have sexual relations--without using effective
birth control--they have no specific plans for establishing
an independent family unit at the present time.   Audrey
states that both of them continue to date others.   Lucius
has expressed interest in marriage, but Audrey believes
she is not ready for it.   Her mother discourages marriage
to Lucius for she holds the boy in low esteem.   The couple's
get-togethers are marked by arguments and quarrels.

Although Audrey did not want the baby at first, she
has grown to love her, while Lucius was happy with the
baby's arrival and shows affection for her.   Audrey's mother
has now accepted this granddaughter, in spite of her disap-
proval of the pregnancy.

Mrs. P. , Audrey's mother, is a widow and has been
receiving aid from the County Welfare Board for herself and
her twelve children living at home.   The County Welfare
Board has assumed responsibility for the baby's support until the young father becomes financially independent and will
be able to assume the responsibility.   Lucius is enrolled in
a work-training program and will accept employment when
he completes his training.

B.   Individual Behavior and Adjustment

Audrey was born in February of 1948, in Alabama
but came to Newark three years later.   She is the second
oldest among four sisters and eight brothers.   Her father,
who had worked as a welder, died in 1961.   The parents

had enjoyed a stable relationship and she and her many siblings got along well in a home where mutual support was the
norm.   For ten years this family has occupied a flat above
a store in a depressed area of the city.

Audrey attended high school and pursued a general
curriculum, leaving during her senior year after she became
pregnant.   She is an attractive girl and makes an intelligent
impression, her well-groomed appearance marred only by a
missing front tooth.   In the interview she revealed educational interest and aspirations as well as an interest in mu-
sic and teenage parties.

The present child care arrangement in which the paternal great-grandmother looks after Rhoda much of the time
satisfies Audrey, for it leaves her free to pursue vocational
training.   She believes the baby is receiving good care;
Audrey's mother, however, cautions her daughter against
leaving Rhoda too frequently with relatives, lest the attach-
ments she will form will preclude her return to her mother.

Lucius, the baby's father, was born in March, 1947.
He is the oldest of three children, two boys and one girl.
His parents are separated, but the father, who is a vocational school teacher, continues to support his family.
Lucius did not like school and was constantly in trouble
there.   He left after completing the ninth grade and is now
receiving on-the-job training in an industrial plant under a
government program.   His attendance is irregular, and he
evinces the same negative attitude toward job training as
toward education.   He is a nice-looking, athletic boy, apparently concerned about his clothes, who seemed to lack
self-confidence and feel uncomfortable in the presence of
the social worker.   He walks with a slouch and speaks in-
distinctly.   His mother guides him and usually makes decisions for him which he generally accepts, although he re-
sponds with sullen anger.   Mrs. P., Audrey's mother, believes that Lucius treats her daughter badly and is abusive
towards her.

C. Care and Training of Children

Rhoda was born in January, 1965.   She was not seen
by the interviewer, but the following information about her
development and care was obtained from her mother.   She
does not adhere to a regular schedule but eats often and

goes to bed late. She drinks whole milk and takes vitamins and has received two of her immunization shots, one from the Baby-Keep-Well Station and the other from a private pediatrician.

Audrey said the baby does not lack clothes, but frequent laundering is necessary to keep her clean. Audrey hopes to start toilet training as soon as Rhoda starts walking. She has no ideas or opinions concerning discipline. At the time of the interview the baby was left most of the time in the care of the father's grandmother. Periodically, Audrey as well as Lucius' own mother will look after her.

D. Social Activities

Although the P. family, with whom Audrey and her baby were living at the time of the first interview, is not engaged in any formal activities, Mrs. P. has evinced an interest in social and recreational clubs and has asked for suggestions for some low-cost group activities for her younger children. As for Audrey and Lucius, they date others in their circle of friends as well as each other.

E. Economic Practices

This large family unit (Audrey, her mother, her younger siblings, as well as her older sister and her child) all receive assistance from the County Welfare Board. The older sister has worked sporadically but, dissatisfied with earnings of less than $80.00 a week, is usually unemployed. Audrey's mother receives $276.00 monthly from OASI and $230.00 from the Welfare Board.

Mrs. P., an attractive and young looking woman, manages the money; she pays the rent and takes care of other financial obligations when she receives her check, and purchases the staple food supplies needed for the month (e. g. canned food, rice, beans, cornmeal, etc.) She also buys canned milk to replace fresh milk for which she lacks cash at the end of the month. Since her freezer space is limited, she finds it necessary to purchase meat two to three times a week.

Furniture is needed badly, and Mrs. P. says she tries to buy something for the house each month. She has

to buy used furniture, but since she is unwilling to accept
used mattresses she has purchased new ones for which she
pays monthly.   There is no insurance, no savings, and no
hospitalization.

F. Home and Household Practices

This large family occupies a five-room apartment
over a store in a segregated Negro slum area.   They have
lived here for ten years, and efforts to find other housing
have been unsuccessful because of the large number of children in the family.

The physical condition of the home is extremely poor,
with falling plaster and large holes in the walls.   The whole
apartment is in need of insect extermination, painting, and
repairs.   With the exception of the kitchen, all rooms are
used as bedrooms, and still there is not enough sleeping
space.   In the front and back of the apartment old fashioned
coal stoves provide some heat in the winter, but the middle
rooms of this cold water flat are unheated.   There is a used
radio and television but very few toys.

The kitchen was as clean as could be expected in
view of its dilapidated condition.   The family eats in shifts,
with those who attend school eating first and the others later.
Mrs. P. attempts to vary the menu and follows the food suggestions of the dietician in the Head Start program, using
peas and beans as meat substitutes, for instance.   The cloth-
ing supplies for this family are not adequate.   Wash is done
daily at a laundromat across the street.   The older children
all share the housekeeping chores which include floor scrub-
bing, cooking, and ironing.

G. Health Conditions and Practices

The members of this household appeared to be in
good health.   Clinics are used whenever possible, including
the dental clinic at a public hospital.   The whole family received oral polio vaccine.

H. Use of Community Resources

Mrs. P. urges her children to stay in school and

wants Audrey to return to school and graduate, as did the
oldest daughter.   The youngest child attends the Head Start
program.   For health care this family makes use of clinics,
hospitals, and occasionally a private physician, and all family members are conscientious about keeping appointments.
The family receives assistance from the County Welfare
Board.   They would like to move into a housing project, but
have not been able to procure an apartment.   Recreation
agencies have not been used in the past, but Mrs. P. indicated interest in the Boys' Club and the Police Athletic
League when told about them.

Miss P. and her daughter are a structurally incom-
plete family, dependent on the maternal family of origin.
The parents of the young mother, southern Negroes who had
come to the North some 14 years earlier in search of a
better life, headed a relatively stable and solidary family.
The death of the father, who had been chief wage earner,
increasing economic need, and slum living weakened this
family's ability to socialize the children.   Audrey is the second of the older girls to bear an out-of-wedlock child, while
there is a third daughter, who is married and the mother of
three children.

On the surface, Audrey and her daughter Rhoda, do
not present a picture of serious malfunctioning.   They live
in a home which, in spite of its poor physical makeup, offers acceptance and emotional warmth.   The baby is receiving adequate physical care at the home of the paternal
great-grandmother when Audrey is at work, and the young
mother seems very devoted to the child.

Yet, the dynamic aspects of the family picture look
much less promising.   Audrey's ability as a mother has not
been tested nor is it clear at this point who will ultimately
assume responsibility for the child.   Audrey continues to en-
gage in sexual relations with Lucius without using adequate
birth control, making a second out-of-wedlock pregnancy
likely.   Although continuing a close physical and social relationship with him, she is ambivalent about marriage and
her own mother advises against a permanent liaison.   The
young woman's immaturity and the absence of a specified
home for Rhoda make the future of this two-person family
most uncertain.   The poverty, crowding, and dilapidated
condition of the P. home make it an unsuitable place to
rear the child.   In short, the P. case is one in which actual or potential problematic functioning in the relationship

areas is matched by instrumental problem functioning.

Pattern of Intervention

Intervention in the P. family was designed to remedy a decidedly problematic situation. Although prevention is characteristically viewed as intervention before the emergence of serious problems, this case offers an opportunity for preventive service because of its great potential for further deterioration.

In the early research interview Audrey was tactful and cooperative in arranging to be privately interviewed. The social worker also found her cooperative in treatment. Yet, the girl's youth, her general immaturity, and her lack of experience in child rearing made it necessary for the worker to be in frequent contact with her, her boyfriend, her mother, and collateral agencies. Over the 14 month period covered in the present treatment report, the worker had 38 in-person contacts with the client and various members of her family, or 2.7 such contacts per month. Twenty-seven took place in the client's home, eight in the office, and three at agencies where the worker had taken the client. In addition, the social worker made 66 phone calls to the client, her family, or collaterals. Initially, Audrey was seen alone or with other members of her mother's household, but as she and her boyfriend moved toward a decision to marry, the two were seen jointly as well as separately. During the last period of treatment covered in this study, as Lucius attempted to assume financial responsibility for the family, he was seen alone a number of times in succession. Contacts were initiated by the worker, as against the client, at a ratio of 5 to 1, and that ratio remained fairly constant throughout services. The modes of intervention covered the gamut of techniques identified for purposes of this study, particularly exploration, discussion, advice and guidance, use of community resources, and practical help. The complexity of this case with regard to the involvement of agencies and extended family made it necessary for the worker to balance discussion with the client with an active exploration of the attitudes and feelings of everyone concerned. Work with community resources and the rendering of personal services of various kinds were made necessary by this family's very limited ability to cope with health, economic and housing problems.

A tabulation of the subjects dealt with in treatment interviews shows complete coverage of all areas of family functioning, with a particularly heavy emphasis on provisions for income (the project supplied emergency funds on eight occasions to help the family out of tight spots), budgeting, job training, housekeeping practices, and contraception.

Because of the P.'s poverty and their lack of skill in finding jobs and contacting community resources, treatment had to be concentrated in the instrumental areas of family functioning. Yet, intra- and interpersonal problems of family members called for the continued exploration and discussion of family relationships and individual behavior as well. When it became clear that Lucius would continue to be associated with the family, the father's potential role as family head and wage earner, his lack of education and inability to hold a job became a special focus of intervention. So did the interpersonal problems which arose after the couple began living in the same household.

Preventive intervention in the P. case required the social worker to concentrate initially upon the physical and emotional welfare of Audrey and her infant, helping the young mother work out plans which could lead to a more stable and secure social situation for them both. With the emergence of the new family configuration, the behavior of the father and the relationship between the parents became significant foci of services, while the need for instrumental help continued unabated.

Changes During Treatment

About half a year after the start of treatment and following the birth of the second child, Audrey and Lucius K. were married. Audrey, who had initially resisted marriage, yielded to the cumulative pressures of pregnancy and birth and the urging of friends and relatives, including her own mother who had changed her mind on the subject. Following marriage, husband and wife continued living in their parental homes for two months, then temporarily moved in with Lucius' family of orientation until they could secure an apartment in a public housing project.

During the period preceding the second pregnancy and marriage, Audrey continued working in the Youth Corps program but dropped out before completing training as a result of her mother's urging that she assume greater responsibility for Rhoda. Yet, the paternal grandmother, who had been caring for the child, continued to provide most of the care for her. The parents, the social worker observed, tended to view the baby as a plaything, buying her presents and adopting very permissive child rearing practices.

Lucius, when employed, contributes money to his mother's household in return for her periodic care of Rhoda. His employment pattern is erratic, and he is equally irregular in attending a vocational training program for which he receives pay. Despite his inadequate income, he frequently makes extravagant purchases.

The establishment of a joint household in the home of Lucius' mother has created new problems for the young couple. They disagree on budgeting and spending, with Audrey manifesting a more realistic and less impulsive approach than Lucius. They have trouble communicating with one another, and Audrey is using her mother-in-law to intercede with her husband to achieve her goals. Their sexual adjustment, however, is satisfactory. Now that the nuclear family is living together as a unit, Audrey devotes much time to the children, and both parents exhibit warmth and affection toward them. There is some friction between Audrey and her mother-in-law, the former resenting the latter's suggestions about child care but following them, nonetheless. All in all, Mrs. K., Lucius' mother, appears to be a stabilizing influence because of her considerable personal maturity and experience in most areas of family life. Beyond that, Audrey is the more decisive voice in such family affairs as handling finances and dealing with community agencies.

Lucius sometimes takes over housekeeping functions, particularly when Audrey feels too overwhelmed by their financial problems and lack of resources for keeping the family going. She is aware of Lucius' poor employment record but does not consider herself able to effect changes in it.

The young couple and their children moved to a two bedroom apartment in a public housing project when this became available. After an eight weeks' stay with Lucius' mother, she supplied the young family with the bulk of the secondhand furniture which now fills their apartment. Audrey and Lucius have, however, acquired a new bedroom

set and are paying for it on the installment plan.   Their social life continues to be intertwined with the extended family,
particularly the K.'s, Lucius' relatives.   He, in return, continues his dependence upon his mother, and his salient role
in the situation is that of a son rather than husband and
head of family.

Four months after moving to their new home and at
the end of the treatment period covered in this report, Audrey gave birth to a third child, a son.   Her attempts to prevent conception by using birth control pills--supplied by
Planned Parenthood--had failed, mainly because of irregular
use.   Lack of planning and poor judgment also characterizes
her functioning in other areas.   She does not, for example,
leave instructions for sitters when she needs to be away
from home; she makes gifts to relatives and friends, thereby
compounding her family's financial problems; she fails to
seek needed medical service.   In contrast, she does respond positively to direct guidance and is more likely to follow through when the action comes close upon the heels of
advice.

At the end of the service period covered in this report, the young K.'s live as a nuclear family in their own
household for the first time; it appears that a measure of
family stability has been attained.   However, the foregoing
analysis makes it clear that the family situation is precarious at best.   Family pressures as well as supports and the
social workers' service, involving frequent contact with both
husband and wife, are factors which keep the family functioning.   It would be difficult to assess the effect of professional service by itself.   Continued intervention will address
itself to the question of whether the present family constel-
lation constitutes an adequate ground for the welfare of family members and the socialization of the children.   One of
the major functions of professional service is the assessment of the present or alternative social structures to
achieve these goals and the rendering of service toward their
achievement.

Notes

1.   This information is based largely on the research
      interview prior to the start of services.

2.   Bruce Lagay and L. L. Geismar, "The Treatment
        Log - A Recording Procedure for Casework Practice
        and Research." New Brunswick, N. J. , Graduate
        School of Social Work, Rutgers-The State University,
        1967.   (Mimeographed.)

3.   On some home visits more than one person was seen,
        alone or jointly with another.

Chapter 5
From Remedial to Preventive Intervention

Social work and the other helping professions in the
human behavior areas have failed, by and large, to provide a
clear definition of the parameters of their services or treatment. Such definition should include the types of behavior,
situations, and problems that must be dealt with; the methods and techniques for dealing with them; the specification
of goals to be attained; and the assessment of outcome relative to these goals. The operation of most agencies, clinics, and welfare institutions provides testimony to the fact
that the fields of social work, clinical psychology, and psychiatry rarely make serious efforts toward achieving definition of objectives.

The reasons for this situation are many and complex,
and they are outside the framework of the present study.
It is clear, however, that the very conditions which make
it difficult to specify behavior, method, goals, and outcome
in the remedial services which constitute the bulk of helping service are also operating--perhaps to an even greater
extent--in a preventive service endeavor. Remedial or rehabilitative services are clearly problem-oriented. Although
the causes of the problems may be difficult to identify and
may be beyond the range of current professional knowledge,
the existence of these problems makes it possible to define
conditions or situations that require intervention. This, in
turn, can serve as a clear focus for treatment planning as
well as for assessing treatment results.

Preventive intervention, by contrast, involves insti-
tuting services to deal with problems which have not yet occurred or which have not yet become a serious threat to
family welfare and unity. Such a goal requires service
planning based on a knowledge of probable developments in
family functioning. Prognostications about probable developments take the form of statistical predictions derived from
longitudinal or controlled cross-sectional studies, of which
the foregoing example might be considered a prototype.
Forecasts about probable developments may also represent

111

inferences about the future based on an analysis of the
present situation, inferences based on research knowledge,
practice experience, intuition, or perhaps a combination of
these.

Whatever the nature of the data used for preventive
service planning, they are at this time, with our present
state of knowledge about human behavior, more imprecise
than problem-focused date relating to present functioning.
This does not detract from the validity of the preventive approach; it merely points up some of the difficulties inherent
in putting preventive intervention on a scientific footing.
The challenge for producing objective evidence of the feasibility and utility of preventive intervention rests in the hands
of the researcher. Hypotheses on the efficacy of preventive
services will need to be subjected to rigorous testing by
means of longitudinal and experimental design.[1]

Even assuming a high rate of research activity in
preventive intervention, scientifically derived practice knowledge will be slow to accumulate. Practice in the meantime
will need to draw on good diagnostic data of individual cases
and practice wisdom in general in order to develop a service strategy which can stand up under the rigorous tests of
utility and effectiveness.

The foregoing three cases illustrate ways in which
prevention approaches can develop at various levels of social functioning. With the accumulation of knowledge--
from repeated cross-sectional and longitudinal studies--on
the development of family functioning, strategies based on
the case approach can become anchored in an empirically
derived theory of family change.

In the G. family, the social worker sought to identify areas of vulnerability in which the family would be likely
to experience stress in social functioning, particularly in
the triangular wife-husband and (his) mother relationship.
The treatment focus arising from this observation did not
represent a special kind of foreknowledge or insight that
might not be present in remedial practice. Rather, the
preventive aspect of service to the G.'s was that families
such as this one are not considered in need of professional services. To the extent that comparative data on the life-cycle
stage might have provided any guidelines to patterning intervention, one would have based it on a prediction of greater
likelihood of deterioration in individual behavior and expres-

sive, rather than instrumental, areas of functioning (see Table 15) in this lower middle-class family.

The social functioning profile of the B.'s, a lower-class family, had revealed acute problems in the instrumental areas of income, health, and housing. These also happen to be the areas of greatest vulnerability for Class V and VI families as they get older. Particularly in the B. case, intervention to increase and stabilize family income was designed to reduce the gap between growing financial need and the inadequate and inflexible relief budget. It is this gap which constituted a serious threat to family welfare and stability.

With the P.'s, another lower-class family, intervention in instrumental areas had to be matched by a concerted effort to assist the members of this poorly defined procreation unit to acquire an identity as a family and to stabilize reciprocal relationships. One of the more promising aspects of intervention in the P. situation resided in the fact that treatment could be given at a time when, because of the youth of the children, the patterns of social functioning had not deteriorated to a stage of "clear and present danger."[2]

In the three family situations preventive action operates within the context of three distinct levels of social functioning, and each of these corresponds to differing measures of problemicity. At the lower, more problem-ridden levels, prevention is not applicable in the pure sense of the definition given earlier, i.e. intervention before the appearance of problems or at the point where problems are beginning to emerge. The B. and P. families do not fall into these categories. Although differing substantially in type and severity of problems, both cases revealed easily identifiable patterns of malfunctioning. In such a situation the prevention concept can be rationalized on two levels, the first of which we shall label developmental and the second provision of services.

Within the developmental context it can be argued with some conviction that young families, such as the sample cases, with only one infant at the onset of treatment have not unloosed the negative potential inherent in personality or environment for the rearing of children. The argument is based on the yet to be proven supposition that in such situations as are illustrated by the B.'s and P.'s, the family's progression through the earlier stages of the life cycle is closely correlated with an increase in malfunctioning.

The provision of services argument connects the definition of prevention with the availability of services to meet emerging or future needs. If available services are geared only to deal with problematic situations, any special treatment aimed at conditions of lesser urgency could be termed preventive. This relativism cannot be carried too far lest any form of service short of treatment to cope with severe pathology and disorganization be classified in the preventive category. From the point of view of professional expectations, provisions for remedial intervention must be put at a level--and for preventive intervention above that level--where the social and emotional welfare of the people themselves are adversely affected. The precise cut-off point for service eligibility and availability is bound to vary from community to community, depending on local standards and resources. However, remedial services come into play at the point at which psycho-social functioning becomes stressful to some persons or groups in the community.

On the basis of general professional expectations in the service area where the study was done, the P. family represents a case of clear-cut professional responsibility for a number of purely remedial services, while other services rendered by the project were outside the community mandate. As for the B. family, it might be argued that the relatively high degree of famiy stability suggested merely the rendering of better provisions for family income and health but obviated the need for other remedial professional intervention. Project services in the psycho-social area were thus largely preventive. At the time preventive services were being initiated to the G. 's they were unlikely candidates for referral to any existing problem-focused professional helping service.

There is need for some agreement as to when a service may be considered preventive or remedial. In using the concept prevention a useful distinction can be made between the purpose of the service and the service's actual effectiveness. If a service is aimed at a population group whose members function by and large above the level where professional standards would make intervention mandatory, the purpose of the service is essentially preventive. Conversely, service aimed at coping with functioning which by professional standards is viewed as problematic can be defined as remedial. Any given cross section of the popula-

tion served is likely to contain a proportion of cases like
the P.'s whose need for remedial intervention can be clearly established.   Can service to them also be considered
preventive?   This question must be answered in terms of
the long range effectiveness of the service.   Within the
framework of definition of purpose, service to problem-ridden families like the P.'s can only be characterized as
remedial.

When we attempt to define prevention in terms of effectiveness, the issue becomes more complex.   To establish that a service is an effective preventive agent it must
be shown (1) that without the service there would be a decline or deterioration in the quality of social functioning,
and (2) that the service acts to prevent or retard that process.   Both types of evidence can best be furnished with the
aid of statistical techniques.   An answer to the question is
intervention with any particular family--whether functioning
adequately like the G.'s or poorly like the P.'s--preventive,
can be given only in probabilistic terms.   The framework
for judging such outcome is created by means of research
knowledge about the natural development in social functioning of groups of families found originally at diverse levels
of functioning adequacy.   Information compiled on changes
in functioning without professional intervention can be expressed as probabilities of finding given types of change
(e.g. improvement, no change, deterioration) in family functioning.   A specific type of outcome resulting from the rendering of services can then be interpreted relative to the
probable changes in family functioning in the course of natural, untreated family development.   An ultimate decision
on the effectiveness of a total preventive service requires
a test of the significance of difference in change patterns
between family groups which received and those which did
not receive intervention.   The effectiveness of prevention is
established if natural development represents a trend toward
greater malfunctioning and intervention can be shown to have
had the effect of significant modification of this trend in the
direction of greater adequacy.   When this can be shown,
service can be defined as preventive for it has served to
either retard or prevent probable deterioration in the family
situation.

The foregoing makes it obvious that a major research
effort is required to establish the validity of preventive intervention on a scientific basis.   One may question whether
the present scientifically underdeveloped state of social work

services does not make such an effort impossible. Will not
the difficulties bound to occur in developing scientifically
grounded preventive efforts only serve to perpetuate existing
patterns of service which operate without accountability?
It might be argued that remedial or rehabilitative social
work needs to establish itself scientifically before the social
work profession can seriously invest its efforts and resources in preventive intervention. Such reasoning postulates that preventive intervention needs to build on scientifically based remedial intervention before it can establish itself on a sound professional footing. However, that supposition is not convincing simply because at this point in time
factors other than scientific rigor influence the growth of the
social work profession; scientific method can at best seek to
catch up and run along with the growth process since it does
not yet determine its course.

Although we have argued earlier that preventive intervention at this stage has not identified techniques differing
from those used in problem-oriented or rehabilitative social
work, the significant contrast with the more traditional forms
of helping lies in the social context within which it operates.
The very fact that prevention is administered prior to or at
an early stage in the development of patterns of malfunctioning, influences the meaning of services to both giver and re-
ceiver. One is left to speculate at this point about the manner in which this affects attitudes and motivations.

In our society problem-oriented services dealing with
psycho-social functioning--and the bulk of services are prob-
lem-oriented--carry a high degree of stigma,[3] adversely affecting the client's attitude toward treatment. Stigmatization
may lead to a complete avoidance of services or to such resistance that service is quite ineffective. The result of a
client's negative attitude toward treatment is likely to be reflected in the attitudes and behavior of the professional staff.
Psychiatrists, clinical psychologists and social workers in
voluntary agencies tend to take a dim view of the client who
is not motivated to seek help because of a preconceived notion that he will not benefit from treatment. Such a view
tends to favor service to the self-referred and the motivated
in preference to those who do not come by choice and may
be most in need of help. One can scarcely doubt that the
net effect of stigmatization will be reduced demand by potential consumers, diminished client satisfaction, and, most
probably, the lessened effectiveness of treatment.

In all likelihood, the stigmatization of professional helping may be reduced by institutionalizing services on a preventive rather than a remedial level. Institutionalization implies, of course, that services become established and accepted as endeavors serving total populations such as communities or neighborhoods rather than groups of socially handicapped individuals. One could visualize preventive intervention in psycho-social functioning resembling routine health checkups at clinics or the office of private physicians. Like such medical services, preventive social agencies could be used for remedial as well as preventive purposes. Universal usage by cross-sections of the population would tend to create a more favorable image for services than that now resulting from limiting them to those who have problems.

To become widely accepted, a preventive service must be institutionalized within the broad framework of consumer services--such as education, health, legal aid, recreation--which are available to the total population. The British Citizens' Advice Bureau[4] possesses many of the characteristics recommended here for a preventive service. The British CABs, says Mildred Zucker, "have evolved from an emergency general service in times of crisis to an 'everyman's adviser' in normal times."[5] Such a conception of service, if shared by the public, can spell the difference between ready acceptance and stigmatization. Acceptance can be furthered by adopting a number of other properties which characterize the CAB's such as ready accessibility, an open door policy barring none, a wide range of services which include referral to specialized agencies, and, above all, service to all social classes, all ethnic groups and all religious groups represented in the service area.[6] It would be advantagous to locate an agency providing preventive intervention in a neighborhood center or a community school.

Agencies or centers for preventive services instituted in the near future are not likely to control evaluative research facilities which can test whether prevention goals are being attained. Yet, even in the absence of a more refined research technology, the coming of preventive services can be marked by a new approach to goal setting, the study of service input, and the assessment of results relative to set goals.

Alfred Kahn's monograph on Neighborhood Information Services proposes a provocative list of agency functions[7] which may be differentiated by determining whether

intervention calls for simple information giving and guidance
or more complex assistance; requires a referral or service
by the agency itself; or necessitates simple advice giving or
actual counselling and treatment, be it short term intervention or continuing services based on a reaching-out approach. [8] The classification furthermore distinguishes between services aimed at modifying the behavior of or the
relationships among individuals by education or therapeutic
techniques and services attempting to modify the environment by seeking policy changes in agencies and services,
conducting programs of education, and promoting the self
organization of people with common problems.

It should be possible to classify families which have
made contact with the services in terms of level of social
functioning and type of issue or problem on which intervention should be focused and to relate both of these to the
function or functions which were found to be most helpful in
dealing with each situation. The detailing of specific functions relative to client situation results in the formulation
of a treatment goal which again may be as simple as providing advice on steps which will force the landlord to turn
on the heat in cold weather or as complex as dealing with
a family situation characterized by multiple problems in
personality, relationships, and instrumental functioning.
There should then be a formal assessment of change in functioning and its relationship to treatment goals at the termina-
tion of services.

The concept of task, advanced recently by Elliot
Studt as part of a larger effort aimed at researching and
reconceptualizing social work practice, [9] appears uniquely
appropriate for a framework of preventive intervention in
social work with families. "The more general meaning of
task for social work," Studt observes, "assumes both a common goal for the worker and the client and different kinds
of sub-tasks for each."[10] The concept task thus furnishes
a common denominator for future actions of family members and professionals rendering preventive services.

The term task also brings under one heading a variety of related worker duties or sub-tasks such as diagnosis,
setting treatment goals, method of practice, technique of
service, and evaluation. These in turn are related to the
family tasks or psychological, social, and economic functions which confront the client family. The family's functions are also composed of various sub-tasks which, ideally,

are formulated to correspond to the need of the family to
maintain or improve its social functioning.   Task in the
above context represents a series of diverse but correlated
assignments for both the family and the intervening agent.
The task concept lays the groundwork for a client-worker
partnership in which the expected and actual contribution of
each can be identified, articulated, and evaluated.   This
partnership, while important to all social work, becomes
crucial in preventive intervention.

To begin with, the family which is not beset by serious problems will probably respond less affirmatively to a
one-sided therapeutic approach than to a service which is defined as a joint enterprise between worker and client.   Furthermore, for the family with an orientation toward prevention the concept of task is seen to comprise the notion of
developmental task. [11]   Family developmental task gives rec-
ognition to the responsibility every family faces for preparing for successive stages of family development.   These
family tasks change in keeping with the changing needs of
family members and the respective expectations of society
at various life-cycle stages. [12]

The planful anticipation of and preparation for future
family roles and family functions are not only theoretically
the central focus in preventive intervention; they are also
motivationally, for the client, one of the most acceptable
rationales for receiving services.   The developmental task
approach permits the family and the social worker mutually
to stake out time periods, task areas, and task goals, the attainment of which can be observed and evaluated systemati-
cally.   Evaluation will not merely concern itself with the
question of where has the family gone during a given time
period.   Evaluation will also assess the degree to which
workers and family members have accomplished their respective sub-tasks.

A client follow-up several months after the conclusion
of services to learn whether any treatment gains have been
maintained poses no formidable technical problems, particularly if clients had been told during treatment that the procedure is a standard concomitant of services rendered.   In
assessing treatment outcome it is more advantageous to employ a classification scheme which correlates the level of client functioning prior to treatment with task goals and attain-
ments as well as with client movement than it is to use an
undifferentiated method which relates treatment goals to cli-

ent movement without regard to the client's level of functioning and the reciprocal performance of tasks.   An agency
with a wide range of services, envisaged here, provides an
opportunity to study the relative effectiveness of intervention at diverse levels of social functioning and at different
stages of the individual and family life cycles.   Short of
studies employing an experimental design, comparative data
from many agencies on outcome along the foregoing lines
can yield converging evidence on the value of a preventive
approach in psycho-social functioning.

     This report has concerned itself with the changing
character of social functioning during the early phases of
the family life cycle.

     A comparison of cross-sectional data gave support
to the hypothesis that young families tend to function less
adequately as the family increases in size and children
reach school age.   At the same time it was noted that these
so-called developmental changes vary with social class and
that extensive deterioration in instrumental areas as well
as the overall situation occurs more characteristically in
lower-class families.   The apparent trend in family functioning toward greater problemicity offers the challenge to
intervene early, at a point of lesser malfunctioning.   The
hypothesized utility of such an approach is in need of empirical testing.   Arguments advanced here in favor of early
and, hopefully, preventive intervention are supported by
analogies from the fields of medicine and public health.   In
the absence of empirical evidence about the validity of the
preventive approach, discussion was focused upon the assumed advantages of services extended to the total community or neighborhood which are not stigmatized by exclusive
identification with the psycho-socially handicapped.

     For the most part, the subject of prevention has been
dealt with on a theoretical level.   The practical implication
of the foregoing research and discussion is a recommenda-
tion for research and demonstration projects which will test
the soundness of prevention in social work.   Such endeavors
could become extensions of and adjuncts to well established
services--rather than independent terminal operations--
thereby insuring continued professional assistance to those
who need it after the project has terminated.

     A shift from the remedial to the preventive approach
requires a substantial reorientation for both social workers

and the users of their services. It is clear that the former are charged with providing the leadership and education
that is required. The latter will respond if the service is
highly visible, readily accessible, courteous, comprehensive
in the sense of addressing itself to a wide range of consumer needs, and, above all, if it meets their needs. For
those who supply social work services, this means adopting
a service philosophy that diverges from that now guiding the
dominant service patterns of the profession.

Affirmation of a preventive approach in social work
is largely dependent on a change in the overall conception
held by American welfare leaders and policy makers about
the role of social welfare. Prevention, according to Kahn,
is more in line with the institutional rather than the residual view of social welfare. [13] The residual conception has its
roots in American welfare history as well as in the dominant socio-religious ideology of the American people. [14] The
idea of welfare as a basic institution charged with serving
all the people has been gaining ground since the 1930's.
But in spite of gradual gains in support of an institutional
approach to welfare, the predominant concept continues to be
residual.

If social welfare is recognized as comparable to education and health in meeting the normal needs of individuals
and groups, the idea of prevention will no longer appear as
remote as it is at present. One may object that health,
though far from being a residual institution, is not--except
for public health--prevention oriented. Although the medical profession tends to favor greater emphasis on preventive
medicine, especially for population and age groups that are
vulnerable to disease, curative medicine has been operating
from a position of strength because of its impressive suc-
cesses in helping people. Social work can make no similar
claims and, therefore, stands less to lose and hopefully
much more to gain by trying a fresh approach.

Social work might find it profitable to model itself
more closely after education and public health, two institutions which are thoroughly prevention-oriented. Few parents
challenge the right of schools to educate and, in a broader
sense, to socialize their children, nor do they question the
utility of well-baby clinics or of regular medical and dental
checkups at public schools. Because of society's greater
acceptance of preventive intervention in education, schools
might be the natural institution in which social work can

move from a preoccupation with children in trouble to one
of promoting the psycho-social health of the children and
their families.

Information derived from this study suggests that
preventive services might usefully concentrate on the family,
especially the young family, for three reasons: (1) social
malfunctioning as a seemingly cumulative phenomenon related to the family life cycle makes prevention feasible;
(2) preventive intervention could reach several people at a
time; (3) social work practice is sufficiently broad and di-
versified to deal with the many and varied needs of families.

Need patterns, as the previous analysis has shown,
vary from one family to the next, but they also show common characteristics when grouped by life-cycle stage, class,
type of community, and possibly other unexplored dimensions
such as: family composition, ethnic group, nature of family
network, etc. Effective service planning should be aimed
at attaining a degree of specialization within the need range
of a well defined population. Such an arrangement is prefer-
able to one by which a preventive service seeks to meet--
by direct intervention or referral--the most variegated needs
of families in a heterogeneous community. It may be assumed that a degree of specialization in function not only
makes for greater administrative efficiency but also greater
effectiveness in service.

Service rendering on a neighborhood basis offers one
approach to developing patterns of professional functions
which are especially attuned to the needs of population sub-
groups. In serving lower-class areas, however, the advantages of serving homogeneous populations may be outweighed
by the disadvantage of ghettoizing services. If there is a
danger that this might happen, efforts should be made to
locate services so that families of higher status groups are
served together with those of lower status. This can be arranged by compromising on specialization, i. e. serving perhaps two or even three socio-economically homogeneous
population groups rather than abandoning the approach altogether. Neighborhood centeredness of services makes it
possible to examine and treat family need within the total
social context of neighborhood living, taking into account
values and expectations, needs and problems, patterns of
organization and social services. A preventive service in
a population area where the services are not meeting the
people's need may have to address itself more forcefully to

efforts at modifying services than at changing behavior.
The converse may be true in a neighborhood with adequate
social resources. A neighborhood-based service operates
from a vantage point where it is able to assess service gaps
and spearhead action from the problem source.

In the American community the first task of an agency
offering preventive services would be that of legitimizing itself in the neighborhood.   This requires a major public relations effort aimed at gaining the cooperation of prestigious
and established institutions such as churches and synagogues,
boards of education, medical organizations, labor unions,
ethnic associations, etc.   Even though such an agency would
devote itself, among other things, to dealing with family
problems and family pathology, the emphasis in public relations should be on the educational and developmental functions rather than that of problem-solving.   Such an approach,
as stated earlier, would minimize the social stigma attached
to the total service and thereby also lend an improved image to the remedial services.

Our analysis of a cross-section of families strongly
supports the contention that the main thrust in giving service, allowing for some class variation, would be on (a)
helping families become more effectively related to their environment and (b) dealing with minor intra-familial problems
arising out of the normal developmental processes such as
child birth, changing jobs and homes, school attendance,
adolescence, etc.   Families, especially young families,
make very limited use of community resources, [15] partly because they do not know about these resources and partly because those that exist for lower-class families, such as public assistance, child welfare, and clinic services, are unsatisfactory and stigmatized, hence used only in dire emergency.   Hopefully, a neighborhood-wide preventive service
might become a major resource which could give direct aid,
and could play the role of advocate, i. e. help families get,
from existing resources, the services they need and to
which they are entitled.

A neighborhood-wide preventive service can strengthen
its operation by mobilizing neighborhood support and direction through the establishment of a board that is representative of the population served.   This kind of board can play
a crucial role in attracting potential users of services, especially in lower-class neighborhoods where there is a great
cultural gap between the professional personnel and the people

to be served. [16] The task approach proposed above lends itself particularly well to efforts aimed at agency-consumer planning not only at the case level but also at the policy level.

In conclusion it should be reiterated that preventive intervention is not to be viewed as a nostrum for all the problems of the profession. The claims for this study are more moderate. It produced some empirical support of the theoretical premises which link family life cycle with changes in social functioning. This tentative finding sets the stage for advocating the testing of the hypothesis, derived mainly from the field of public health, that early intervention into psycho-social functioning can become preventive intervention. A beginning treatment model built on analysis of a sample of young families was drawn up and three case illustrations from an ongoing research action project were discussed.

Objective evidence is yet lacking on the validity of the preventive approach in social work. While research now in progress holds out hope for providing empirical support to the aforementioned hypothesis on prevention, other arguments, largely outside the framework of the present study, have been cited in favor of institutionalizing preventive programming. These arguments affirm the probable advantages of a shift in professional service from a remedial and rehabilitative approach to one predicated on prevention. Two major benefits discussed were (1) the lesser stigmatization inherent in a neighborhood-wide service which plays down the problem-solving function and highlights educational and developmental tasks, and (2) the opportunity to lend to preventive service wide neighborhood support through the cooperation of accepted social institutions and the establishment of a policy making board representing the potential consumers of services.

It is conceivable that these and other conditions attendant upon a smooth process of institutionalizing the proposed services may have greater and more favorable effect on the outcome of the preventive approach than treatment factors related to timing and technique of intervention. But this premise, too, charged as it is with possibilities for the development of the profession, is in need of testing in the arena of action as well as the sphere of research.

Notes

1. As an example see L. L. Geismar and Jane Krisberg, "The Family Life Improvement Project; An Experiment in Preventive Intervention," Social Casework, Part I, Vol. XLVII No. 9, Nov., 1966, pp. 563-70; Part II, Vol. XLVII No. 10, Dec., 1966, pp. 663-667.

2. This expression has been used to denote a situation in which the welfare of one or more persons or a group is being threatened to the extent that the community has a right to intervene.
See Alice Overton and Katherine H. Tinker and Associates, Casework Notebook. St. Paul, Minn., Family Centered Project, 1957, pp. 1-10.

3. The term stigma is used here to denote "an attribute that is deeply discrediting." See Irving Goffman, Stigma. Englewood Cliffs, N. J., Prentice-Hall, Inc., p. 3.

4. Mildred Zucker, "Citizens' Advice Bureaus: The British Way," Social Work, Vol. X, No. 4, Oct., 1965, pp. 85-91; Alfred Kahn et al. Neighborhood Information Centers. New York, Columbia University School of Social Work, 1966. pp. 16-36.

5. Zucker, loc. cit., p. 86.

6. Kahn, et al. op. cit. pp. 35-36.

7. Ibid., pp. 112-119.

8. The categories are not necessarily mutually exclusive and are cited as a suggested approach to the development of a typology of interventive functions in a broad gauged program of intervention.

9. Elliot Studt, Sheldon L. Messinger, and Thomas P. Wilson, C-Unit: Search for Community in Prison. New York, Russell Sage Foundation, 1968.

10. Elliot Studt, "Social Work Theory and Implications for the Practice of Methods," Social Work Education Reporter, Vol. XVI, No. 2, June 1968, pp. 22-46, p. 24.

11.   Reuben Hill and Roy H. Rodgers, "The Developmental Approach," in Handbook of Marriage and the Family, Harold T. Christenson, editor. Chicago, Rand McNally and Co., 1964, pp. 171-211.

12.   Ibid., pp. 190-202.

13.   Alfred J. Kahn, "Therapy, Prevention and Developmental Provisions, A Social Work Strategy," loc. cit., p. 137.

14.   Wilensky and Lebeaux, op. cit., pp. 138-140.

15.   Greenleigh Associates found in Detroit that needed and relevant services were not used because people did not know about them. Study cited by Kahn et al., op. cit., p. 61.

16.   The question of residents' participation in neighborhood services is discussed in chapter 6 of Robert Perlman and David Jones, Neighborhood Service Centers. Washington, D. C., U. S. Department of Health, Education, and Welfare, Welfare Administration, 1967. pp. 54-62.

Index

Agency functions, 117, 118; see also Preventive services

Alienation, and intervention, 74-75; as a variable, 48, 51; related to Srole Anomie Scale, 47

Anomie Scale of Srole; see Srole Anomie Scale

Areas of family functioning; in table, 61; see also Family functioning, Categories of

Attitudinal correlates of family functioning, 47-52

Beck, Bertram, 13

Birth control, 34, 35, 46

Blood, Robert O. and Wolfe, Donald M., 17

Boehm, Werner W., 13

Bross, Irwin D. J., 68

Chemung County Research Demonstration, 29

Child socialization, as a variable, 50, 51; related to PARI scales, 47, 48; related to intervention, 78

Chilman, Catherine S., 47

Church attendance, 35

Citizens' Advice Bureau, Britain, 117

Client-worker relationship, reorientation, 120, 121

Commission on Social Work Practice, NASW, 13

Data, collection of, 26-27, 29, 47; reliability and validity, 29, 30

Deprived families, 78; intervention with, 78, 79

Developmental task, 118, 119

Diagnosis, of family, 69

Divorce rates, 17

Educational approach, in intervention, 74

Evaluation of marriage, 46, 51

Family disorganization and early intervention, 16, 18, 19; and family life cycle, 17; growth of, 17, 18; indices of, 15, 17; prevalence of, 15

Family functioning, categories of, defined, 30-34, 73, 74, 77, 78; related to St. Paul Scale, 14, 15, 30-34; relevance of intervention, 72-80, 112-115

Family goals, 35; in intervention, 72, 73, 76, 77

Family Life Improvement Project of Rutgers-The State University, 14, 25, 59, 76, 83, 90

Family of orientation, social functioning of, 43-45, 51

Family of procreation, social functioning of, 43-45, 51

Health problems, 34

Herzog, Elizabeth, 42

Hill, Reuben, 80

Hollingshead Index of Social
Position, 36
Hunt-Kogan Movement Scale,
29

Intervention: early, defined,
19; in case studies, 90,
91, 98, 99, 106, 107, 112-
115; strategies with Ade-
quate or Near Adequate
families, 72-74; Near
Problematic families, 74-77;
Problematic families, 77-
80; see also Family dis-
organization and intervention

Kahn, Alfred J. , 13, 14, 117,
121

Length of engagement, 45,
46, 51

Marital status, 40, 41, 51
Marriage age, 46
Migration, 46
Moynihan Report, 42

Neighborhood information services, 117
Neighborhood based services,
122

Parad, Howard, 72
PARI scales, 27, 47-51, 78;
content of, 47-48
Patterns of family functioning: see Family function-
ing
Persistence prediction, 68, 69
Porterfield, John D. , 13
Prevention: in social work,
13, 14, 16; meaning, 11,
13-15, 111; public health
model, 13, 14; with mal-
functioning families, 113,
114; see also Preventive
intervention

Preventive intervention, basis
for planning, 68-70; cen-
tral focus, 119; knowledge
basis, 111, 112, 115, 116;
see also Prevention
Preventive services: acceptance of, 117; and social
welfare, 121; effect on stigmatization, 117, 123, 124;
effectiveness, 115; in neighborhoods, 122-124; models,
121, 122; outcome, 83, 84;
specialization of, 122; to
young family, 122; see also
Intervention, Prevention,
and Preventive intervention
Problemicity, 69, 70; treatment focus, 69
Profiles of agency clients, 59
Public health; approach, 72;
model, 13, 14

Race: related to family func-
tioning, 42, 43, 48
Random sampling technique:
limitations, 67
Rapoport, Lydia, 14
Remedial services, 111, 114
Research designs, limitations,
67, 68
Residence: and family func-
tioning, 37-40, 48
Rutgers University: see Fam-
ily Life Improvement Pro-
ject of Rutgers-The State
University

St. Paul Scale of Family Functioning, 14-15, 27, 29, 30,
33
Social class: as a variable,
37-43, 45, 46, 48, 50, 51,
62-67; related to intervention, 69, 70, 75-77
Social-Economic class: see
Social class
Social functioning: adequacy
defined, 15; educational

approach, 74; enhancement of, 74; in families, 29-35, 59-67

Social status: see Social class

Social welfare: institutional conception, 121; residual conception, 121; treatment approaches, 121

Social Work Curriculum Study, 13

Social worker: roles, 70, 71; role model, 78; treatment strategies, see Intervention, Prevention, and Preventive intervention

Srole Anomie Scale, 27, 47

Studt, Elliot, 118

Study populations, 25, 26, 59

Task: as social work concept, 118, 119

Treatment Log, 91

Treatment planning: developing a model, 19, 20; see Intervention, strategies

Wolfe, Donald M.; see Blood, Robert O.

Young families: developmental changes, 120; social characteristics, 27, 28; social functioning, 29-35

Younger and older families compared: social functioning, 59-67

Zucker, Mildred, 117